Trilogy on Faith and Happiness

The Augustine Series

Selected writings from "The Works of Saint Augustine—
A Translation for the 21st Century"

Volume VI

Trilogy on Faith and Happiness

Trilogy on Faith and Happiness

Augustine of Hippo

Translated by
Roland J. Teske, S.J.
Michael G. Campbell, O.S.A.
and Ray Kearney

Introductions and notes by
Michael Fiedrowicz
and Roland Teske, S.J.

Edited by
Boniface Ramsey

New City Press
Hyde Park, New York

Published in the United States by New City Press
202 Comforter Blvd., Hyde Park, NY 12538
www.newcitypress.com
©2010 Augustinian Heritage Institute

Cover design by Durva Correia

Library of Congress Cataloging-in-Publication Data:

Augustine, Saint, Bishop of Hippo.
 [Selections. English. 2010]
 Trilogy on faith and happiness / Augustine of Hippo ; edited by Boniface Ramsey.
     p. cm. — (The Augustine series ; v. 6)
 Includes bibliographical references.
 ISBN 978-1-56548-359-0 (pbk. : alk. paper) 1. Faith—Early works to 1800. 2. Happiness—
Religious aspects—Christianity—Early works to 1800. I. Ramsey, Boniface. II. Title.

 BR65.A52E6 2010d
 234′.23—dc22   2010024753

2nd Printing: February 2018

Printed in the United States of America

Contents

Preface

The three treatises brought together in this volume, *The Happy Life*, *The Advantage of Believing*, and *Faith in the Unseen*, are a sampling from the early works of Augustine, written before he achieved the theological confidence that a careful study of the epistles of the Apostle Paul was eventually to give him.

The Happy Life was composed during the autumn of 386, after Augustine had decided upon being baptized (which took place at the following year's Easter Vigil) and while he was staying at a friend's villa at Cassiciacum, not far from Milan. Here he spent several months in the midst of a close-knit community of family and friends, including his mother Monica, his son Adeodatus, his brother Navigius, two cousins, Lastidianus and Rusticus, two students, Licentius and Trygetius, and his close friend Alypius. Augustine reports on the lengthy discussion or dialogue which considered the question of the pursuit of happiness. Happiness, he notes, is linked to the desire for good things that can never be lost. Monica plays a key and forceful role that is hardly in keeping with her limited educational background, and concludes that "unhappiness is nothing but neediness." Augustine identifies happiness with the possession of wisdom, which is none other than the Son of God. *The Happy Life* is notable for, among other things, its very sparing use of scripture.

The second work in chronological order is *The Advantage of Believing*, written immediately after Augustine's unexpected ordination to the priesthood in Hippo in 391. Augustine dedicated the work to an old friend, Honoratus, with whom he had been heavily involved in the Manichean movement. Here Augustine defends the Catholic interpretation of the Bible and finds proof of

7

the Church's authenticity in its reputation, the number of its followers and its diffusion throughout the world. In the face of the Manichean attack on the supposed credulousness of Christians, Augustine uses the example of friendship and familial relations to show how faith is indispensable in everyday life. He also discusses miracles and notes that, if they were more frequent, they would cease to amaze and astonish us, although in fact everyday existence is replete with miracles associated with the annual seasons. Lastly, Augustine insists that religion does not belong exclusively to the intellectually elite, as is indicated by the uneducated masses of men and women of many nations who believe and preach it.

The authenticity of the last work, *Faith in the Unseen*, has been debated by scholars because it does not appear either in Augustine's *Revisions* or in the list of Augustine's works assembled by his biographer Possidius and known as the *Indiculus*. Nevertheless, a strong argument for its authenticity is found in Letter 231 (7), addressed to Augustine's friend Darius, where a work with the same title is mentioned. This treatise must have been composed soon after 399. Here too Augustine speaks of the indispensable role of faith in human life. Human beings must by necessity believe in many things which cannot be seen, in particular the trust and good will of friends and, even more so, of spouses. Those who allege that faith in Christ lacks proof are greatly mistaken, as seen in the fulfillment of Old Testament prophecy, while the truth of the Church's teachings is evidenced by the fact that it is spread throughout the world.

These three works bear witness to a writer who moves step-by-step through his arguments in a way that is intentionally easy for his reader to follow, and all three give special weight to the rational pursuit of truth.

Daniel E. Doyle, OSA
Villanova University

The Happy Life

Translation, introduction and notes
by Roland J. Teske, S.J.

Introduction

The Happy Life is one of the first two writings of Augustine to have survived. He wrote it in the fall of 386 at the villa of his friend, Verecundus, a Milanese teacher of grammar, at Cassiciacum near Milan, in sight of the Alps. During the previous summer Augustine had discovered the books of the Platonists and achieved the insight that allowed him to think of God and the soul as non-bodily substances. Up until that point his thinking was dominated by the prevalent Stoic corporealism of the West, which held that whatever is not a body is not real. Without the ability to conceive of a non-bodily substance Augustine had been unable to extricate himself from the Manichean challenges to Catholic Christianity about the source of evil in the world. For the Manicheans shared the corporealism of the Stoa and concluded that, if evil is to be real, it must be a bodily substance. Augustine had spent over nine years as a "hearer" in the Manichean sect, and his exposure to the books of the Platonists, that is, the *Enneads* of Plotinus and possibly some works of Porphyry, provided him with the intellectual tools to free himself definitively from the snares of the Manicheans and to begin to develop a spiritualist metaphysics that provided him with a much more adequate understanding of the Christian faith. In Milan he had come into contact with a group of Christian Neoplatonists, which included their bishop, Ambrose; Simplician, who would be Ambrose's successor; and Manlius Theodore, to whom Augustine dedicated *The Happy Life*.

Augustine remained at Cassiciacum until the beginning of Lent in 387, when he submitted his name as a candidate for baptism. At the Easter Vigil on the night of April 24, 387 he was baptized

11

in Milan along with his son, Adeodatus, and his friend, Alypius, who was soon to become the bishop of their hometown, Thagaste.

Many aspects of Augustine's conversion in the years 386 and 387 remain matters of scholarly debate, but the claim made early in the twentieth century by Prosper Alfaric and others, that Augustine was at this time converted to Neoplatonism rather than to Catholic Christianity, has been effectively countered by the discovery of a circle of Neoplatonist Christians in Milan.[1] Augustine was not converted either to Neoplatonist philosophy or to the Catholic faith but to both, and he used features of Neoplatonist thought to come to an understanding of the Christian faith that would dominate Western thought from the fifth century to the present, barely rivaled only by the Thomistic synthesis of the thirteenth century.

By its very title *The Happy Life* announces a theme that is present in many of Augustine's writings and that remained a central concern of his to the end of his life. Like all ancient thinkers, Augustine was convinced that the desire for happiness or the happy life was universal. Like all Christian thinkers, he was convinced that happiness was ultimately attainable only in the enjoyment of God. The whole purpose of philosophizing was, Augustine maintained, the attainment of happiness,[2] and the whole purpose of worshiping the true God was the attainment of the happy life, as Augustine insists again and again in *The City of God*.[3]

1. The Structure and Content of the Work

The Happy Life begins with an introduction (sections 1 to 6) and is followed by a discussion that is spread over three days. Sections 7 to 16 contain the discussion that was held on the first day, Augustine's birthday, sections 17 to 20 the discussion that

---

1. See Prosper Alfaric, *L'évolution intellectuelle de Saint Augustin I: Du Manichéisme au Néoplatonisme* (Paris 1918) for the claim that Augustine was converted to Neoplatonism in 386-387 rather than to Christianity. See Pierre Courcelle, *Recherches sur les Confessions de Saint Augustin* (Paris 1968) on the existence of the Milanese circle of Neoplatonist Christians.
2. See *The City of God* XIX, 1.
3. See, e.g., *The City of God* V, 1.

was held on the second day, and sections 21 to 36 the discussion that was held on the third day.

In his introduction Augustine develops an elaborate image of the human soul as cast onto the stormy sea of this life and trying to make its way to the harbor of philosophy from which it may disembark onto the land of the happy life. The initial question is whether more human souls would make their way into the harbor of philosophy and to the land of the happy life, which is their heavenly fatherland, if reason and will set the course for them. As it is, Augustine admits, only a few now arrive there. Augustine is puzzled at how souls came to be in this predicament on the stormy sea of this life and suggests that "either God or nature or necessity or our own will or some or all of these in combination have cast us forth into this world, . . apparently without purpose or plan" (section 1). At times, however, a storm forces one into the harbor of philosophy, even though at the time the bad weather seems to be only a hindrance for one's travel. Augustine sees three sorts of human beings sailing on the stormy sea of life whom philosophy can welcome. A first group, which is sailing only a short distance offshore, can make an easy landfall and become a signal light for others. A second group is lured farther out to sea by the enticements of the world and moves farther from their fatherland, often forgetting it. These persons need a storm to drive them into the harbor from which they will not again emerge. A third group remembers its fatherland and either seeks it immediately or delays for a time and then is forced by some disaster back to its homeland (section 2). Within the harbor of philosophy there is a mountain of vainglory from which proud philosophers can point the way to the happy life, but they can also lure some to their proud peak and the destruction it entails (section 3).

Augustine then addresses Manlius Theodore. He describes his own life from the time he read Cicero's *Hortensius*, his long commitment to Manicheanism, his brief dalliance with the Academic skeptics, his recent contact with the spiritualist thought of Ambrose and of Theodore himself, and his present state of mind after having discovered the books of Plotinus. He tells Theodore how he compared the books of Plotinus with the Christian books and how he was inflamed with the love of philosophy, though he still needed a problem with his health to drive him into philosophy's arms (section 4). Though he is now sailing in the harbor of Neoplatonic philosophy, as Theodore can see, Augustine asks for Theodore's help in order that he may enter upon the land of the happy life, where Augustine believes that Theodore already dwells (section 5). Hence, Augustine offers Theodore the present work in order to reveal his current thoughts and disposition and in order to obtain Theodore's assistance in finding the land of the happy life. He explains to Theodore, who had not been present at Cassiciacum, the context in which the discussion there about the happy life took place and the persons participating in it (section 6).

Augustine now recounts for Theodore the discussion itself that was held on the topic of the happy life at Cassiciacum. It begins when he gets his partners in conversation to admit that we are composed of body and soul and that the food we eat is for the body rather than for the soul (section 7). Minds, however, have a food and nourishment of their own, namely, intellectual knowledge, and those minds that lack such food are starved or filled with defects and vices (section 8). Hence, Augustine proposes to set forth a banquet for the mind on his birthday, though he warns that only healthy minds will enjoy such food (section 9). He states, and everyone else agrees, that we all want to be happy and that no one is happy if he does not have what he wants. And yet not everyone who has what he wants is happy. For, as Monica is quick to point out, a person is only happy if he wants and has good things. Licentius asks Augustine what the good things are that we should want and desire, but Augustine sets aside his request for the time being (section 10).

Augustine then gets his companions to agree that everyone who is not happy is unhappy and that everyone who does not have what he wants is unhappy. Furthermore, in order to be happy one should want to have something that he can have when he wants it, that is, "something that lasts forever and is not dependent on good luck or subject to misfortune." Hence, what we should want cannot be something mortal or perishable. Though some people

have all the goods of fortune that they want, they cannot be satisfied by them; hence, they are always in a state of want. A person
who sets a limit for himself in such possessions would be happy
not because of such possessions but because of the moderation
of his mind. All agree that in order to be happy one must want
and have something that he cannot lose against his will, that is,
something eternal and imperishable, and that only God is such.
Hence, they agree that whoever has God is happy (section 11).
The question then becomes: Who has God? and three answers are
proposed: first, that he has God who lives a good life; secondly,
that he has God who does what God wants; and thirdly, that he
has God who does not have an unclean spirit (section 12). Having
obtained these answers, Augustine suggests that his companions
should not overindulge on his birthday but should continue the
conversation the following day. In drawing the day's discussion
to a close, however, he suggests an idea that seems to resolve
the problem posed by Academic skepticism in the *Answer to
the Skeptics*, the conversation that began just before *The Happy
Life* and was continued after it (section 13). After all, if no one
is happy who does not have what he wants and if the skeptics are
always seeking the truth, but do not find it, they cannot be happy.
Furthermore, the skeptics claim that their wise man is happy, and
yet he cannot be happy since he does not have what he wants
(section 14). Licentius refuses to accept the argument, but Augustine shows him that the conclusion follows inevitably from what
seem to be undeniable premises (section 15). Since some of the
group were not involved in the discussion about the Academics,
Augustine explains to them who these skeptics are and eventually
gets everyone to assent to the argument. Then they adjourn for the
day (section 16).

The discussion on the second day takes up the three responses
to the question as to who has God (section 17). Augustine shows
that a person who lives a good life is someone who does what
God wants and that a person who does not have an unclean spirit
is someone who has no sin, so that the three expressions turn out
to be equivalent (section 18). He then introduces a new question,
namely, whether God wants us to seek him, and all agree that he

does. But he then points out that a person who seeks God does what God wants, lives a good life, and does not have an unclean spirit. Since, nonetheless, a person who seeks God does not as yet have God, it is not true that a person who does what God wants, lives a good life, and does not have an unclean spirit immediately has God. Monica again intervenes, claiming that everyone has God, but that someone who lives a good life has God as a friend, while someone who lives a bad life has God as an enemy. Augustine observes, however, that in that case not everyone who has God is happy (section 19). In fact, it would seem that not even everyone who has God as a friend is happy; otherwise, one would have to admit that someone who is still seeking and therefore does not have God is happy. Even someone, then, who does not have what he wants would be happy—contrary to what the group had agreed to on the previous day (section 20). Again Monica comes to the rescue with a distinction between having God and not being without God. Thus, someone who lives a good life has God as a friend, while someone who lives a bad life has God as an enemy, and someone who is still seeking God does not have God either as a friend or as an enemy but is not without God. Augustine objects that God is a friend to someone he favors and that he favors someone who is seeking him. Hence, a person who is still seeking God has God as a friend and is happy. Hence, it follows that a person who is still seeking and does not have what he wants is happy. Monica again intervenes and claims that not everyone who has God as a friend is happy, but that only someone who has already found God has God as a friend and is happy (section 21). Augustine, however, points out that they had granted that everyone who is not happy is unhappy, from which it follows that someone will be unhappy even though he has God as a friend, since he is still seeking God and, therefore, cannot as yet be happy. Here a large lacuna is found in the text, as Augustine himself acknowledges in the *Revisions*.

The discussion resumes with a question from Cicero, quoted by Augustine. Cicero asks whether we should call wealthy land-owners happy and the possessors of the virtues poor. Augustine wonders if it is true that every needy person is unhappy and that every unhappy person is needy, which would mean that unhappiness was the same as neediness. But since this is a big question, the group adjourns for the day with the agreement to gather again on the morrow (section 22).

The third day begins with bright sunlight, and the group meets outdoors. Augustine tells his companions that one question remains, namely, whether all unhappy persons are needy. For, if they are, then a person without need will turn out to be happy (section 23). Trygetius suggests that they can conclude that everyone who is not needy is happy from the fact that everyone who is needy is unhappy. Augustine points out that the conclusion does not have to follow as Trygetius has suggested (section 24). Augustine explains that everyone in need is unhappy and that the bodily needs of a wise person do not undermine this position, for the happy life is found in the mind, which is perfect and needs nothing. The mind of someone wise takes what the body needs if it can, but it does not want such things if it cannot have them. Hence, nothing happens against the will of a wise person (section 25). Then he raises the question as to whether everyone who is unhappy is in need. The difficulty with this view is that some people who have a great abundance of the goods of fortune still have a difficult life; that is, though they need nothing, they are unhappy. The example of Sergius Orata, a wealthy and cultivated Roman cited by Cicero, is used to show that even such a man, with all his blessings, would still be unhappy, since someone with his intelligence would have to fear that he would lose these goods (section 26). Licentius points out that, though Orata was in fear, he was not in need. Hence, not everyone who is unhappy is needy, since Orata was unhappy because of his fear, not because of his need. Again Monica intervenes, pointing out that, though Orata had such great riches and wealth that he desired and needed nothing more, he was in need of wisdom if he feared losing what he had. Pleased with his mother's insight, Augustine remarks that, though she lacks all sorts of learning, she still has her mind set upon God, from whom she derives such knowledge (section 27). Augustine concludes that neediness of the mind is simply folly, which is the opposite of wisdom, with nothing in between. Hence, Orata was unhappy because he was a fool. And if he did not fear to lose his possessions, he would be secure only due to his deeper folly (section 28).

Since Trygetius did not quite follow the argument, Augustine runs through the premises again to show him that neediness is simply another name for folly, and he takes the opportunity to point out that to have need is not to have something positive but is simply to lack something. Hence, he concludes that unhappiness is the same as neediness (section 29). Next Augustine asks who is not in need, for a person who is not in need will be both wise and happy. Folly is a sort of neediness, and Augustine points to the wisdom of the ancients, who coined at least the most important words, recalling from the conversation on his birthday that "wickedness" (*nequitia*) in Latin is derived from "not anything" (*nec quicquam*) and that its opposite is "fruitfulness" (*frugalitas*); in the latter two terms we see being and non-being, or a positive reality and a lack. Augustine brings his companions to agree that the opposite of neediness is plenitude, just as the opposite of poverty is wealth (section 30). Hence, Augustine argues that, if neediness is folly, plenitude will be wisdom. He appeals to Cicero, who had identified fruitfulness with moderation and temperance and called it the greatest virtue (section 31). Moderation is, he points out, derived from "limit" (*modus*) and temperance from "harmonious balance" (*temperies*). He notes that where there is limit and balance there is neither too much nor too little, and that this is precisely what plenitude connotes. On the other hand, anything that is too much or too little is in need at least of a limit. Furthermore, the limit of the mind is wisdom, whose opposite is folly. Since folly is neediness, it turns out that wisdom is plenitude, which has a limit. But, he adds, the mind's limit is wisdom, and he cites the famous Stoic motto, "Nothing to excess" (section 32).

At the beginning of the third day's discussion the group had agreed that, if they discovered that unhappiness was neediness, they would admit that a man without need was happy. Hence, they conclude that to be happy is simply not to be needy, that is, to be wise. And wisdom turns out to be the limit of the mind by which it remains in balance so that it does not run into excess or fall short of fullness. Hence, the mind ought to direct itself toward wisdom and not turn toward distractions or the deception of images. A person, then, who is happy has his limit (section 33).

Though up until now there have been only a few hints that the wisdom and limit of the mind that Augustine has been speaking of are anything more than the great Stoic virtues that were qualities of the mind, he now identifies wisdom with God's wisdom, that is, with the Son of God, who is, of course, God. Hence, a happy person has God, as everyone had agreed at the beginning. Wisdom is, moreover, the truth that comes to be through some highest limit from which it proceeds and to which it returns. Thus the highest limit turns out to be the Father, who is known through the truth, that is, through the Son. As the truth has never been without the limit, so the limit has never been without the truth. That means, in the language of the Council of Nicaea, that they are consubstantial. For minds to have God is for them to enjoy God (section 34). Furthermore, Augustine continues, there is a certain warning that leads us to remember, seek, and thirst for God and that flows from the fountain of the truth to us. This warning is also clearly God, perfect and without any diminution in perfection. As long as we are still seeking and have not quenched our thirst with plenitude, we have not arrived at our limit. Hence, we are not yet happy and wise, for the full satiety of minds, which is the happy life, consists in knowing perfectly the warning that leads us to the truth, the truth that we enjoy and that unites us to the highest limit. For those who understand, Augustine says, this is God. Monica recognizes here the Trinity and bursts out with the first verse of Ambrose's hymn to the Trinity, adding that this is the happy life to which we can be brought by faith, hope, and love (section 35). Finally, in order that their banquet may have a limit, Augustine thanks God and his guests for their gifts and contributions to their conversation and brings the discussion to a close (section 36).

2. The Text Translated and Other Translations

The Latin text that has been used for this translation is found in the Corpus Christianorum Series Latina XXIX, 65-85. *The Happy Life* has been translated into English many times, most recently by L. Schopp in The Fathers of the Church I (1948) 43-84, and by M. T. Clark in *Augustine of Hippo: Selected Writings* (Paulist Press 1984) 163-193. It has been most recently translated into French by J. Doignon in Bibliothèque Augustinienne IV/1 (1986) 131-152; into Italian by D. Gentili in Nuova Biblioteca Agostiniana III (1970) 183-225; into German by I. Schwarz-Kirchenbauer and W. Schwarz in *Über das Glück* (Stuttgart: Reclam, 2006); and into Spanish by V. Capánaga in Biblioteca de Autores Cristianos I (10) 522-666.

Revisions I, 2

One Book on the Happy Life

It happened that I wrote a book on the happy life not after the books on the Academics but while I was occupied with them. It was begun on the occasion of my birthday and was completed after three days of discussion, as it itself quite clearly indicates. In this book we who were searching together[1] agreed that there was no happy life apart from the perfect knowledge of God. I regret, however, that in it I made more of Manlius Theodorus, to whom I dedicated the book, than I ought to have, although he was a learned and Christian man; that I also often referred to fortune in it;[2] and that I said that the happy life resided only in the mind of a wise person during his own lifetime, in whatever state his body might be,[3] although the Apostle hopes for the perfect knowledge of God—meaning that than which nothing can be greater for a person—in the life to come,[4] which alone can be called the happy life, when the incorruptible and immortal body[5] will be subordinate to its spirit without any disturbance or reluctance.

As a matter of fact I found this book incomplete in our codex and containing less than it should, and that is how it was transcribed by some of the brothers; even to this day I have not found a complete copy of it with which I could make corrections when writing these revisions.

This book begins in this way: "If ... to the harbor of philosophy."

---

1. I.e., the group of persons who were with Augustine at Cassiciacum.
2. Ibid.
3. 4,25.
4. See 1 Cor 13:12.
5. See 1 Cor 15:53.

The Happy Life

1, 1. If a course set by reason and will led men to the harbor of philosophy[1] from which someone could reach the land and territory of the happy life, I do not know, gentle and great Theodore,[2] whether it would be rash for me to say that far fewer men would arrive there. For even now, as we see, only a few exceptional men reach this land.[3] For either God or nature or necessity or our own

---

1. Augustine takes "philosophy" in its etymological sense as the love of wisdom. He distinguishes between the philosophies of this world which the scriptures condemn and the one true philosophy which is found in the Christian religion and in Platonism. See *Order* II, 5, 16. For Augustine "wisdom" is the knowledge of eternal and unchanging things, and both the Platonic philosophers and the Christian religion lead toward this intelligible world beyond time and change. Though a contemporary reader of John's Gospel may be startled by Augustine's interpretation, he does really mean to say that Christ told Pilate that his kingdom was not of this world, thus intimating that it was of another world, namely, that intelligible world of Platonic forms. See *Order* I, 11, 32.
2. Augustine lived at Milan as a close friend of Theodore, to whom the *Revisions* give the first name Manlius. Theodore was consul in 399 and fulfilled with acclaim high functions under several emperors. Claudian wrote a panegyric in verse on his consulate. The dedication of *The Happy Life* shows more deference to Theodore than the dedications of the *Answer to the Skeptics* show to Romanianus, who was a benefactor of Augustine. In fact, Theodore seems to have exercised on Augustine an influence analogous to that of Ambrose. A man of great culture, enthusiastic for Neoplatonism, generous and just, an ardent Christian, Theodore had been for Augustine in his quest for the truth a counselor and support. For that reason the dedication of *The Happy Life* resembles more closely a confession than an exhortation. Augustine wants Theodore to know deeply his life and his present thoughts and wants him to rejoice in the knowledge that his friend has finally, after so many storms, entered the harbor of philosophy.

    In any case, Augustine thought it well, in the *Revisions*, to moderate the praise he gave to Theodore in his dedication. There is exaggeration, he tells us, in the praises that he addressed to Theodore, even though he is a wise man and a Christian. The influence of Theodore could have been important for Augustine, but one cannot in any case compare it with the influence of Ambrose and Monica.
3. In his early works Augustine is convinced that a few men trained in the liberal arts and philosophy could attain a happiness in this life that could not be surpassed even hereafter. In *Order* II, 9, 26, he says, "Few are able to attain such knowledge in this life, but no one can go beyond it even after this life."

23

will or some or all of these in combination have cast us forth into
this world as though upon a stormy sea, apparently without purpose
or plan.[4] This is a question that is very obscure; yet it is one that
you have undertaken to clarify. And so, how many would know
the direction in which they should struggle or the way they should
return if a storm, which the foolish regard as unfavorable, did not at
times force them unwilling and struggling against it into that land
of their great desire while they are wandering in ignorance?[5]

2. I think I see three sorts of men sailing this sea whom philosophy can welcome. The first sort are those who, after reaching
an age in command of reason, flee from a short distance off shore

---

4. Here Augustine suggests that the soul existed elsewhere and came to be in the world
   for one of four reasons, that is, either God or nature or necessity or its own will has
   cast the soul into this world. In *Free Will* I, 12, 24, he says, "But since wisdom resides
   in the soul, it is a great secret and something that we shall have to discuss in its proper
   place whether the soul lived another life before its union with the body." And in *Free
   Will* III, 20, 56-21, 59, he returns to the question of the origin of the soul and articu-
   lates four hypotheses. These are (1) that individual souls are generated like our bodies
   from our parents (traducianism), (2) that they are created anew as human beings are
   born (creationism), (3) that they existed elsewhere and were sent here by God or (4)
   that they existed elsewhere and fell down hither by their own will. Both (3) and (4)
   involve the soul's existing prior to its embodiment. Option (3) makes embodiment
   the result of God's sending the soul into the body, while (4) makes the soul's presence in the body the result of its sin. Augustine treats the question again and again
   during his career, but even at the time of the *Revisions* he still insists, "But as far as
   concerns its origin by which it happens that it is in the body, whether it is from that
   one who was created first when man was made into a living soul or whether individual
   souls are made for individual men, I neither knew then nor know now" (*Revisions*
   I, 1, 3). With regard to this passage, O'Connell has noted that it still remains possible that at one point Augustine thought he knew; see Robert J. O'Connell, *St. Augustine's Early Theory of Man, A.D. 386-391* (Cambridge: Harvard/Belknap, 1968)
   150. See O'Connell's other books and articles, which have amassed a great deal of
   evidence that indicates that Augustine did hold a theory according to which souls
   pre-existed the embodiment into which they fell by sin. But the issue is still disputed,
   and one should consult Gerald O'Daly's rejection of O'Connell's position as well
   as O'Connell's response. See O'Connell's *The Origin of the Soul in St. Augustine's
   Later Works* (New York: Fordham University Press, 1987) for Augustine's changing
   views on this topic before and during the Pelagian controversy.
      Despite his inability to solve the question of the soul's origin, Augustine did come
   to solve some other problems with regard to the soul that had troubled him for years.
   Key to his break with the Manicheans was his discovery of how to think of the soul
   as an incorporeal substance. Moreover, he came to reject the Manichean view that the
   soul was of the same nature as God. He was never in doubt about the creation of the
   soul of the first man by God. His abiding question had to do with the souls of Adam
   and Eve's descendants. On the Manicheans see note 13.
5. During his many years as a follower of the Manicheans Augustine never lost the deep
   conviction that there was a God and that he exercised providential care over humans.
   See *Confessions* VII, 7, 11.

and with a small effort and stroke of the oars settle in that peacefulness. There, for whomever of their fellow citizens they can, they raise up some work of their own as a brilliant signal by which others might be warned and thus try to return to themselves.[6] The second sort, unlike the first, are those who, beguiled by the deceitful face of the sea, have chosen to move out into the middle and dare to wander far from their fatherland and all too often forget it.[7] If a wind which they consider favorable has followed them astern somehow or other and quite disguisedly, they enter the depths of misery elated and rejoicing. For everywhere the deceitful calm of pleasure and honors seduces them. What else should we desire for these men than some failure in those affairs in which they are happily caught up and, if that is too little, a violent storm and a hostile wind which might lead them amid tears and groans to certain and solid joy? Yet several of this sort who have not wandered a great distance are drawn back by lesser troubles. These men wake up somehow or other in the harbor of philosophy when the sad tragedies of their fortunes or the worrisome problems of their empty concerns shove them into the books of the learned and wise as if they had nothing else to do. And from there no promises of that sea with her deceiving smile can lure them back out. Between these there is a third sort: those who either on the threshold of manhood or already tossed about long and much look back and see some signs and remember their dear fatherland even though they are at sea.[8] Then they either seek her again on a direct unswerving course and without delay or (as is more common), while wandering off course amid cloudy skies, either watching falling stars or captivated by some allurement, they put off the

---

6. Augustine himself hopes to become such a beacon for others. The theme of returning to oneself is Neoplatonic.

7. Augustine's use of "fatherland" (*patria*) is reminiscent of Plotinus' words that Augustine was so fond of in *Ennead* I,6 where Plotinus speaks of the fatherland where the Father is. Augustine will tie the Plotinian content with the story of Odysseus and of the prodigal son (Lk 15:11-32), both of whom have wandered from their homeland. Note that some forget the homeland from which they have fallen, while others remember it. But to forget or to remember it implies that one was once there.

8. Like Plotinus, Augustine is convinced that not all souls are equally fallen; hence, the return is easier for some than for others. On this point, see O'Connell, *Early Theory* 188. O'Connell finds in the emphasis upon the salvific function of memory and its connection with the liberal disciplines a sure sign of Plotinian influence; see ibid. 191.

times for good sailing and thus wander longer and also often run
into danger. Often some disaster in their changing fortunes, like
a storm opposing their efforts, forces these men into the peaceful
and most desired life.

3. For all these who are brought in any fashion to the land
of the happy life there is one huge mountain set in front of the
harbor itself. This mountain also creates great difficulties for those
entering and should be much feared and carefully avoided. For it
shines forth and is wrapped in deceitful light, so that it not only
offers itself as a place to dwell for arriving voyagers who have not
yet entered the harbor and promises to satisfy their longing for
the happy life, but it also frequently invites men to itself from the
very harbor and sometimes detains them and delights them with
its height, from which they can look down on the rest. These men,
nonetheless, often warn those coming lest they either be deceived
by the hidden rocks below or think that they can easily climb up to
where they are, and because of the nearness of that land they teach
with much good will the way by which those arriving may enter.
Thus, while they begrudge arriving men empty glory, they point
out the place of security. For what other mountain does reason
want to be understood as something to be feared by those who
are approaching or by those who have already entered philosophy
except the proud pursuit of empty glory that has nothing full and
solid within, so that it pushes under and swallows up those walking on it who are puffed up with pride, and once it has wrapped
them in darkness it snatches away from them the shining home
which they had scarcely glimpsed.[9]

4. So, my Theodore, listen (for I look to you alone and admir-
ingly regard you as most suited for what I desire): hear which of
these three kinds of men has brought me to you and where I think
I now am and what sort of help I confidently seek from you. From
my nineteenth year, when I received that book of Cicero's called
the *Hortensius* in rhetoric class, I was aflame with such a love of

9. See *Confessions* VII, 9, 13, where Augustine mentions that a man swollen with pride
gave him the books of the Platonists, i.e., the *Enneads* of Plotinus. See Eugene TeSelle,
Augustine the Theologian (New York: Herder and Herder, 1970) 33, for attempts to
identify this proud Platonist. Courcelle has suggested Theodore, O'Meara Porphyry,
and Solignac the Celsinus mentioned in *Answer to the Skeptics* II, 2, 5.

philosophy that I planned to devote myself to her immediately.[10] But there was no lack of clouds on my voyage to confuse my course, and for a long while I admit I looked up to stars falling into the ocean and was led into error by them.[11] For a kind of childish superstition frightened me away from the search itself.[12]

---

10. The *Hortensius* of Marcus Tullius Cicero, the Roman statesman, orator and author (106-43 B.C.), had a great influence upon Augustine. The work, which has now been lost except for fragments, many of which survive in the writings of Augustine, was a dialogue on philosophy that contained an exhortation to the life of philosophy. For the history and reconstructed text, see Michel Ruch, *L'Hortensius de Cicéron: Histoire et Reconstitution* (Paris 1958). The work, probably patterned after the *Protreptikos* of Aristotle, which has also been lost, was written in 46-45 B.C.

    Augustine read the *Hortensius* when he was but eighteen and repeatedly mentions its influence upon him. Besides this passage, see *Confessions* VI,11,18:

    > I wondered most of all at how long was that time from my nineteenth year, when I had first been fired with a zeal for wisdom. For then I had determined, if wisdom were found, to abandon all the empty hopes and all the lying follies of my vain desires.

    And *Confessions* VII, 7, 17:

    > Many, perhaps twelve, of my years had flown by since that nineteenth year when by reading Cicero's *Hortensius* I was aroused to a zeal for wisdom. Yet still I delayed to despise earthly happiness, and thus devote myself to that search.

    And in his *Answer to the Skeptics* I, 4, Augustine notes that the *Hortensius* has won over to philosophy the young Trygetius and Licentius. Though Ruch refers to Augustine's reading of the *Hortensius* as his "road to Damascus" (p. 43), that image may be too strong, since Augustine himself would seem to indicate that the fire set by the *Hortensius* was far surpassed by the blaze kindled by the reading of the books of Plotinus. See *Answer to the Skeptics* II, 2, 5.

11. Leo Ferrari suggests that Augustine has adapted a line from Virgil's *Aeneid* (III, 515) and is alluding to the appearance of Haley's Comet over Carthage in early March of 374. Ferrari sees the appearance of the comet as "a decisive factor in Augustine's conversion to Manicheanism" (Leo C. Ferrari, *The Conversions of Saint Augustine* [Villanova: Villanova University Press, 1984] 43). The text, however, seems to imply that Augustine looked to such falling stars prior to his conversion to Manicheanism. Hence, the fog and the falling stars useless for navigation could refer to the obscurantism and anti-intellectual tone of the Church of Africa.

12. Ferrari ties the "childish superstition" to the simple Catholic's reaction to Haley's Comet, for which the Manicheans had a rational explanation. Though that explanation remains possible, it seems more probable that the superstition that Augustine mentions had to do with the anti-intellectual attitude of the Church in Africa which demanded an assent of faith without offering even that minimal explanation of what was to be believed which could assure the believer that he was not being asked to believe the impossible. Thus, in *The Advantage of Believing* 1, 2, Augustine writes to Honoratus, a friend he had led into Manicheanism, that "we fell in with them [i.e., the Manicheans] because they declared with awesome authority, quite removed from pure and simple reasoning, that if any persons chose to listen to them, they would lead them to God and free them from all error."

    He adds that the Manicheans kept saying that they were frightened by a certain superstition and that faith was imposed upon them before reason, whereas they themselves pushed no one to faith, until they had sifted and clarified the truth.

After I had been made more upright, I scattered that fog and was convinced that I should yield to those who teach rather than to those who command, I fell in with men to whom that light seen by eyes was thought of as deserving worship among the highest divinities.[13] I did not assent to this, but I thought that they were concealing something great in their veils that they would sooner or later disclose. But after I shook them off and escaped, especially through having crossed the sea, the Academics long held my ship as I fought against all the winds in the midst of the waves.[14] Finally, I came to this land; here I came to know the North Star to which I could entrust myself.[15] For I noticed often in the dis-

---

See TeSelle 26-27 for evidence that Augustine is referring to the simple faith of African Catholicism when he speaks of "superstition." See also ibid. 132-135 for the conservative character of the African Church.

13. Augustine is referring to the Manicheans, the members of a religion founded by Mani in Persia in the third century. Though Manicheanism was once considered a distinct world religion, it is now recognized to be a Christian heresy, as Augustine always considered it to be. Manicheanism was a universal dualistic gnosticism. That is, it was all-embracing; it held two underived principles, good and evil; and it claimed to provide knowledge rather than to demand faith. According to the revelation that Mani supposedly received, this present world is the product of two principles, one good, the other evil. In the beginning the good principle, the kingdom of light, was separate from the evil principle, the kingdom of darkness, both of which were pictured as vast bodies endlessly extended save where they touched. The offspring of the good principle was in part captured by the forces of the kingdom of darkness, when they did battle. Hence, now in the middle times, bits of the divine light are captured in the darkness of matter. We all experience in ourselves the struggle between our divine soul and our evil body. Eventually in the end times there will again be a complete separation of the good from the evil. Meanwhile, Mani provides knowledge of our present state and prescribes an ethics by which we can free the divine in ourselves from the dark evil of matter. There were two classes of members: the elect and the hearers. Augustine remained only a hearer during his years with the Manicheans. Manicheanism spread rapidly westward into the Roman Empire as well as eastward. Augustine regarded it as the most intelligent form of Christianity when he became a hearer; even later he regarded it as a Christian heresy rather than the separate world religion which it was.

14. The academic skeptics, against whom Augustine wrote his *Answer to the Skeptics*, were the successors to Plato in the Academy and taught that certain knowledge could not be attained and that, hence, doubt or the suspension of assent should be cultivated as the source of peace of mind. Augustine came to doubt that truth was to be found with the Manicheans, while he was convinced it was not to be found in the Catholic Church; hence, he was a natural prey for a school of philosophy that maintained that truth could not be found. See *Confessions* V, 10,19;14, 25. In *Confessions* VI, 4, 6 Augustine alludes to his dalliance with skepticism when he says, "I held back my heart from all assent, fearing to fall headlong, and died all the more from that suspense."

15. The North Star is, obviously, contrasted with those stars falling into Ocean that were useless for steering one's course on the sea of life; it is that point of reference that allows one to steer into the harbor of philosophy. The North Star could here refer to Ambrose, to whom Augustine alludes in the following sentence—and such seems to be the

courses of our priest and sometimes in yours that we should not think of anything bodily at all when we think of God or when we think of the soul, for it is the one thing in reality closest to God.[16] But I was held back, I admit, from flying swiftly into the embrace of philosophy by the enticements of a wife and of honor. I thought that, once I had attained these, I would then at last hasten with full sail and all the oars into that harbor and come to rest there—a blessing that only a few fortunate men attain. However, after I had read a very few books of Plotinus,[17] whom I had heard you were studying, and after I had also compared with these books the authority of those who have handed down the divine mysteries, I so

---

more common opinion—or it could refer to the doctrine that Augustine absorbed from Ambrose, namely, the Plotinian doctrine of the incorporeal nature of God and of the soul, which allowed Augustine to steer a correct course into the harbor of philosophy.

16. The inability to conceive of God or the soul as an incorporeal substance presented Augustine with his greatest metaphysical difficulty, the solution to which he found in the Christian Neoplatonism of the Church of Milan. "I wished to meditate upon my God, but I did not know how to think of him except as a vast corporeal mass, for I thought that anything not a body was nothing whatsoever. This was the greatest and almost the sole cause of my inevitable error" (*Confessions* V, 10, 20).

17. The "very few books of Plotinus" are several of the *Enneads*. It is disputed which of the *Enneads* Augustine read and how early he read them. When Augustine speaks of "a very few books," he ought to be understood as referring to his first soul-stirring contact with Plotinus but should not be taken to imply that he did not go on to read more; see O'Connell, *Early Theory* 8. TeSelle presents a brief history of recent scholarship, showing how the work of Paul Henry and Robert O'Connell has demonstrated that Augustine used more of the *Enneads* than had previously been thought.

TeSelle considers the following *Enneads* as ones that Augustine certainly used:

I, 6: On Beauty
III, 2-3: On Providence
IV, 3-4: On the Soul
V, 1: On the Three Divine Hypostases
VI, 4-5: How That Which Is One and the Same Can Be Everywhere.

TeSelle adds the following *Enneads* as ones that Augustine probably or possibly used:

I, 2: On the Virtues
I, 4: On Happiness
I, 8: On the Origin of Evil
III, 7: On Eternity and Time
IV, 7: On the Immortality of the Soul
V, 3: On the Three Hypostases Possessing Knowledge
V, 8: On Intelligible Beauty
VI, 6: On Numbers
VI, 9: On the Good and the One.

See TeSelle 43-45. On the highly disputed question of how much Plotinus (or Porphyry) Augustine read at the time of his first encounter with the books of the Platonists, see the articles by O'Connell and F. Van Fleteren in *Augustinian Studies* 21 (1990).

burst into flame that I wanted to break all anchors—except that I was still disturbed by what some men would think.[18] Hence, what further resource was left for me, if a storm at sea that I thought unfavorable had not come to my aid as I delayed? Thus such a great pain in the chest seized me that I was unable to carry on the burden of that profession by which I was probably sailing toward the Sirens,[19] and I cast aside everything and brought the shaken and battered ship into that peacefulness that I had longed for.

5. Hence, you can see in what sort of philosophy I am sailing as though in a harbor. That harbor itself is large, and its size does not entirely exclude all—albeit less dangerous—error.[20] For I still do not know which part of the land is alone the land of happiness toward which I should move and where I should disembark. For what do I have that is solid if the question of the soul is still unsettled and up in the air?[21] So I beg you by your goodness, by your kindness, and by our bond of mutual friendship to give me your hand, that is, to love me and believe that you are likewise loved and held dear by me. And if I obtain this favor, I shall arrive with little effort at the happy life itself to which you, I believe, already cling.[22]

---

18. See *Confessions* IX, 2, 2-3, where Augustine tells how he did not want to make an ostentatious break and waited until the vintage vacation to withdraw from teaching. Furthermore, trouble with his lungs necessitated his leaving the teaching profession and provided him with an excuse to do so.

19. The Sirens were the mythical women in Homer's *Odyssey* XII who lured sailors onto the rocks by their beautiful singing. Augustine thinks of himself in images of Odysseus and of the prodigal son, both of whom had wandered away from their homeland and eventually returned.

20. That is, philosophy's harbor is wider than the one true philosophy, which is the Neoplatonic understanding of Christianity.

21. "The question of the soul" most likely refers to the problem of its origin, which Augustine was never able to settle to his satisfaction. But it may refer to the problem of the soul's relation to God, since the Manicheans had claimed that it was divine, or it may even refer to the problem that Augustine had for many years of being unable to conceive of a spiritual substance.

22. The statement that Theodore is already enjoying the happy life is surely one of the reasons that led Augustine in *Revisions* I, 2 to regret the fulsomeness of his praise. On the other hand, at the time when he wrote the early dialogues Augustine did seem to be convinced that one could attain in this life the sort of happiness beyond which one could not go in the hereafter, and he maintained that this happiness was attained through philosophy, so he could very well have thought that Theodore had attained such beatitude. See *Order* II, 9, 26, where Augustine claims that the few, i.e., those trained in the philosophical disciplines, can in this life come to a knowledge of the triune God that is beatific and, even hereafter, unsurpassable. The comment in the *Revisions* is indicative of his having come to realize that no one attains such happiness in this life.

In order for you to know what I am doing and how I am gathering my companions into that harbor, and in order that you may thus more fully understand my mind, I thought that one of my discussions, which in my opinion turned out somewhat more religious and was worthier of your name, should be written down for you and be dedicated to you. For I can find no other signs by which to reveal myself to you. And this is most appropriate, of course. For we have inquired among ourselves concerning the happy life, and I see nothing which might more aptly be called a gift of God.[23] I am not afraid of your eloquence. For whatever I love, though I do not possess it, I cannot fear. Indeed, much less do I fear the height of your good fortune. For, however great it is, in you it is something favorable. For fortune makes favorable those whom she rules. But please be attentive now to what I have to offer.

6. The Ides of November was my birthday.[24] After a modest dinner that would not interfere with our thought, I called together to the baths all of us who were living together not merely on that day but every day. For that place occurred to me as out of the way and suited to the weather. I do not hesitate to make known to Your Graciousness each of them by name.[25] First there was our mother, to whom I owe entirely my life; then my brother Navigius; and also Trygetius and Licentius, fellow citizens and students of mine. And I did not want Lartidianus and Rusticus, my cousins, to be

---

23. Augustine plays upon Theodore's name, which in Greek means "gift of God."

24. In the Roman calendar the Ides fell on the 13th of the month, except for March, May, July and October, when it was the 15th.

25. The cast of characters for the dialogue includes Monica, Augustine's mother who followed him from Africa to Milan. From his nineteenth year Augustine lived with a young woman, who is never named and was the mother of Augustine's son, Adeodatus. When Monica arranged a suitable marriage for Augustine, he sent the mother of Adeodatus away. Since, however, the young woman whose marriage with Augustine Monica had arranged was two years under the legal age, Augustine took another woman for the intervening period. See *Confessions* VI, 15, 25. See *St. Augustine. Against the Academics*, translated and annotated by John J. O'Meara (Westminster, Md.: Newman, 1950), pp. 4-14, for further background on some of the characters in the dialogue. Licentius and Trygetius were two young students whom Augustine was guiding through the *Aeneid* and trying to interest in philosophy. The former was the son of Romanianus, to whom Augustine dedicated the *Answer to the Skeptics*. Navigius was Augustine's brother, while Lartidianus (or Lastidianus) and Rusticus were his cousins. The group had withdrawn from Milan to Cassiciacum, where they lived in a villa provided by Verecundus, a friend and professor of grammar. They left Milan for Cassiciacum in October of 386. See *Confessions* IX, 1,1-6,4 for the months spent there. Augustine returned to Milan to be baptized by Ambrose at the Easter Vigil in 387.

absent, even though they had not yet studied grammar. I thought that their common sense was needed for the matter I was undertaking. There was also present Adeodatus, my son, the youngest of all, but one whose talent, if love does not deceive me, holds great promise.

2, 7. "Does it seem clear to you that we are composed of soul and body?"[26] All agreed, except that Navigius answered that he didn't know. I said to him, "Do you know nothing at all, or should we merely count this point among the other things that you don't know?"[27] "I don't think," he said, "that I am ignorant of everything." "Can you tell us something that you do know?" "I can," he said. "If it isn't too much trouble," I said, "mention something." When he hesitated, I said, "Do you at least know that you are alive?" He said, "I do know that." "Therefore, you know that you have life, since no one without life can live." He said, "Yes, I know that as well." "Do you also know that you have a body?" He admitted that he did. "Therefore, you now know that you are composed of body and life." "I know that, but I'm not sure that these are all there is." "Therefore," I said, "you don't doubt that there are these two, namely, body and soul, but you aren't sure whether something else is needed to make up and complete a human being." "That's right," he said. "What this might be," I said, "let us investigate some other time if we can. Now, since we all admit that there cannot be a human being without a body or without a soul, I ask all of you this: For which of these do we seek food?" "For the body," Licentius said. The rest hesitated and argued among themselves how food could seem necessary for the body when it is sought for life and when life belongs only to the soul.[28] I said, "Do you think that food pertains to that part which we see grows and becomes stronger from food?" They

---

26. See *Confessions* X, 6, 9; *The Catholic Way of Life and the Manichean Way of Life* I, 4, 6.

27. Augustine wants to know whether Navigius is caught up in the problems of academic skepticism so that his claim not to know is just part of a whole philosophical attitude or whether he is merely uninformed on this particular point. The strategy of the rest of the dialogue would, of course, depend upon his answer. *The Happy Life* took place between the discussion of the first book of the *Answer to the Skeptics* and the discussion of the remaining books.

28. Augustine's philosophy of human nature is highly Platonic. A human being is a soul using a body; the soul or mind is the real self and it has come to be in the body to which it gives life and which it uses rightly or wrongly.

agreed, except for Trygetius. For he said, "Why haven't I grown in proportion to my appetite?" "All bodies," I said, "have their own limit set by nature, and beyond that size they cannot develop. Yet they would be smaller than that size if they didn't have nourishment. We readily see this in cattle, and no one doubts that without food the bodies of all animals grow thin." "They grow thin, but they don't get smaller," Licentius added. "For my purposes that's enough," I said. "For the question is whether food pertains to the body. And indeed it does, since without it the body becomes thin." Everyone then agreed that it is so.

8. "What of the soul, then?" I asked. "Doesn't it have nourishment of its own? Or do you think that knowledge is the food of the soul?" "Clearly," my mother said, "I believe that the soul is nourished by nothing other than the intellectual grasp and knowledge of things."[29] Trygetius indicated that he wasn't sure of that opinion, so she said, "Today you showed by your actions, didn't you, where the soul gets its food; for after a considerable part of the meal you said you didn't notice what dish we were using, because you were thinking of other things, though you hadn't held back at all from that part of the meal. So where was your mind when it didn't notice this, even though you were eating? Believe me, the mind is fed by such feasts, that is, by its theories and thoughts, if it can grasp something through them." When they expressed some hesitation about this, I asked, "Don't you grant that the minds of the very learned are much fuller and greater in their own way than those of the uneducated." They admitted that this was clear. "Thus we are correct in saying that the minds of those who are trained in no area of learning and have absorbed nothing of the fine arts are hungry and starved." "Their minds," Trygetius said, "are, I think, full, but full of defects and wickedness." "Believe me," I said, "this condition itself is a sort of emptiness and starvation of the mind. For, as a body without food is generally full of diseases and sores,

---

29. Note that it is Monica who here and elsewhere makes the crucial interventions that move the dialogue along. Augustine tries to portray his mother as one who has attained the very peak of philosophy, though she has not attained this degree of knowledge through instruction in the liberal arts. O'Connell claims that the role Monica plays in the dialogue is fiction and that her interventions are not accurate accounts of what occurred; see his *Early Theory* 229.

and these defects in it indicate starvation, so too the minds of such men are filled with diseases that reveal their lack of food. The ancients decided to call wickedness (*nequitia*) the mother of all defects because it is not anything (*nec quicquam*), that is, because it is nothing.[30] And the virtue opposed to this defect is called fruit-fulness (*frugalitas*). As the latter is derived from fruit (*frux*), that is, from produce, because of a kind of fecundity of the mind, so the former is called wickedness from sterility, that is, from noth-ing. Nothing is whatever is flowing, dissolving, melting, and—so to speak—constantly perishing.[31] Hence, we call such persons lost (*perditos*). Something is, however, if it remains, stands firm, is always the same, as virtue is. And a great and most beautiful part of virtue is what is called temperance or fruitfulness. But, if this is too obscure for you to see, you will surely concede that, if the minds of the uneducated are also full, then there are for souls, as for bodies, two kinds of nourishment, one healthy and beneficial, the other unhealthy and harmful.

9. "Since we have agreed that there are in a human being both a body and a soul, I think that on my birthday I ought to provide a somewhat more sumptuous meal not only for our bodies but for our souls as well. If you are hungry, I shall serve up the sort of dinner this is. For, if I try to feed you against your will or when you aren't hungry, I will be undertaking a futile task and would do better to pray that you desire such meals rather than those of the body. And you will desire them if your minds are healthy. For, as we see in diseases of the body, the ill refuse and spit out their food." All said, the looks on their faces in agreement with their words, that they wanted to take and eat whatever I had prepared.

---

30. Augustine stresses that *nequitia*—worthlessness or wickedness—is derived from *nec quicquam*—not anything. One of his intellectual problems in the preceding decade of his struggle with Manicheanism was the inability to grasp that evil was a privation. Indeed, as long as one thinks that whatever is real is a body, one has to say that evil is a body or is not real. It was only when he was able to think of incorporeal things that Augustine was able to deal with the ontological status of evil. Hence, he now emphasizes this point again and again.

31. Nothing here is obviously something—indeed, it is everything that is not God. As Augustine mentions, it is not easy to grasp what is meant by nothing; see *Order* II, 16, 44. Once he has made the Platonic move of identifying being with the immutable, he has to admit the existence of non-being or nothing. However, this "nothing" is not the nothing out of which God created heaven and earth, as Augustine will come to realize.

10. And so I began once again, "We want to be happy."[32] I had scarcely got the words out when they all agreed. "Do you think that a man is happy if he doesn't have what he wants?" They said, "No." "So, is everyone happy who has what he wants?" At that point my mother said, "If he wants and has good things, he is happy, but if he wants bad things, even if he has them, he is unhappy."[33] I was delighted and said to her with a smile, "Mother, you have indeed reached the very summit of philosophy. For you surely didn't have the words to express yourself as Tully did, but what you've said expresses this thought of his. In the *Hortensius*, a book he wrote in praise and defense of philosophy, he says,

> But notice that it is not philosophers, but those who like to argue, who claim that all who live as they desire are happy. That is surely false. For to desire what one should not is unhappiness itself. And it is not as bad not to get what you want as to want to get what you ought not. For wickedness of the will brings more evil than fortune brings good to anyone."[34]

At these words she cried out so loudly that we completely forgot that she was a woman and would have thought that some great man was seated there with us, while I understood to the extent I could the source—indeed a divine source—from which those words flowed.[35] Then Licentius said, "You ought to tell us what we should want and what things we ought to desire in order that each of us may be happy." "Invite me," I said, "on your birthday, when you want. I will gladly accept whatever you serve. But since you are today my guest for dinner, I beg you not to ask for something I haven't prepared." He was sorry for his modest

---

32. Cicero, *Hortensius*, fragment 36; see *The Trinity* XIII, 4, 7. Like all ancient philosophers Augustine regarded it as obvious that human beings all desire happiness. The only question concerns what it is that makes us happy. In *The City of God* XIX Augustine follows Varro in showing that there are theoretically two hundred and eighty-eight possible different philosophies that are distinguishable on the basis of where one says human happiness lies.

33. Augustine has Monica again intervene at a crucial moment in the dialogue to provide the answer that sets the discussion back on track. Monica has, he claims, attained the heights of philosophy, though she cannot express her thoughts in philosophical language. Monica's words stem not from human learning, but from God.

34. Cicero, *Hortensius*, fragment 39; see *The Trinity* XIII, 5, 8.

35. The divine source is the one teacher, namely, Christ; see *The Teacher* 14, 46.

and discreet suggestion, and I said, "Are we agreed, then, that no one can be happy who doesn't have what he wants and that not everyone who has what he wants is happy?" They agreed.

11. "Well," I said, "do you grant that everyone who isn't happy is unhappy?" They had no hesitation. "Therefore, everyone who doesn't have what he wants is unhappy." All agreed. "What ought a person to try to get for himself in order to be happy?" I asked. "For perhaps this too will be served up at our banquet so that Licentius' craving need not be neglected. For I think that a person should try to get something that he can have when he wants." They said that was clear. "It has to be something that lasts forever and isn't dependent on good luck or subject to misfortune. For whatever is mortal and perishable cannot be had whenever we want and for as long as we want."[36] All agreed. But Trygetius said, "There are many fortunate people who possess in abundance those very things that are fragile and subject to misfortune, though pleasant in this life, and these persons lack nothing that they want." I replied, "Do you think that someone who lives in fear is happy?" He said, "I don't think so." "But can anyone be free from fear if he can lose what he loves?" He said, "He can't." "Yet he can lose these goods of fortune. Hence, someone who loves and possesses these cannot be happy at all." He had no objection. Then my mother intervened, "Even if he is free from fear that he would lose all those things, still he couldn't be satisfied by such things. Hence, he would be unhappy by the very fact that he was always in want."[37] I asked her, "What if, while abounding and reveling in these things, he sets a limit for himself and is content with these things and enjoys them properly and pleasantly—wouldn't you then consider him happy?" She said, "He is happy not because of those possessions but because of the moderation of his mind." "Excellent," I said,

---

36. See *True Religion* 45, 86-88, where Augustine argues that if we want to be unconquered, we must love only what cannot be taken away from us. There he argues that we should not love other human beings because of their bodily and temporal relations to us, which are the result of sin. Rather we should love others as ourselves, i.e., as souls. If we love others as souls, then death cannot separate them from us, especially if we love them in God. On this point, see the beginning of Letter 11 to Nebridius, where Augustine says that he and Nebridius as minds are not separate, though they are separated in place.

37. Here again Monica steers the discussion back on track and introduces the concept of moderation or limit, which will become crucially important in the closing paragraphs.

"and this question deserves no other answer, especially from you. Hence, we have no doubt that, if anyone is determined to be happy, he has to try to get for himself that which lasts forever and cannot be snatched away by any misfortune." "This point," Trygetius said, "we have long before conceded." "Do you think," I asked, "that God is eternal and everlasting?" "That's so certain," Licentius said, "that there's no need to ask." And all the rest piously agreed. "Hence, whoever has God is happy,"[38] I said.

12. They were glad and pleased to hear this; so I said, "Therefore, I think that the sole object of our investigation ought to be: who has God? For such a person will certainly be happy. So I ask you now what you think." Licentius said, "He has God who lives a good life." Trygetius said, "He has God who does what God wills to be done." And Lartidianus agreed with the latter. That youngest lad of all, however, said, "He has God who doesn't have an unclean spirit." Mother approved all of these, but especially the last.[39] Navigius was silent. I asked him what he thought, and he answered that he liked the last one. I didn't think that I should neglect to ask Rusticus for his opinion on this important matter. He seemed to me to be silent more from shyness than from any lack of an opinion. He agreed with Trygetius.

13. Then I said, "I have everyone's opinion on this important matter. Beyond it there is nothing more to seek, and nothing more can be found if only we investigate it now, as we have begun, calmly and sincerely. But it's late today, and minds also have a kind of overindulgence in their feasts if they rush into them beyond the limit and too eagerly.[40] In doing this, they digest their food poorly so that we have to fear for the mind's health on this account no less than from a lack of food. This question, then, will be better for us tomorrow when we are hungry, if you don't mind. Now I should like you to enjoy the taste of something that has occurred to me, your host, to be brought to your attention and that,

---

38. This is the main conclusion of the dialogue, though it still needs to be explicated. In what follows Augustine provides us with an example of an *exercitatio animi*: an exercising of the mind that is meant to prepare the mind for contemplation of God.
39. Monica, the doting grandmother, of course, favors Adeodatus's opinion.
40. Note the repeated mention of "limit" and the theme of moderation. The significance of this theme becomes clear in the final chapters, where Augustine presents his first attempt at formulating an analogy for the Trinity in terms of limit, truth and warning.

if I'm not mistaken, has been mixed and flavored with sweetness like a dessert." When they heard this, they all leaned forward as toward a new dish and urged me to hurry up and say what this was. I said, "What do you think but that the whole business that we undertook with the Academics has been brought to an end?"[41] When they heard this name, the three familiar with the topic jumped up eagerly and, as with hands outstretched, as happens, assisted the waiter bringing in the dish and indicated with what words they could that they would hear nothing with more pleasure.

14. Then I set out the matter as follows. "If it is clear," I said, "that he isn't happy who doesn't have what he wants—a point that reason has just demonstrated—and if no one seeks what he doesn't want to find and if the Academics are always seeking truth without finding it, it follows that they don't have what they want.[42] And, hence, it follows that they aren't happy. But no one is wise if he isn't happy; therefore, the Academic isn't wise." Then they cried out as if they had grasped the whole matter. But Licentius, being more wary and cautious, was afraid to assent and said, "I grabbed it with you, since I cried out and was moved by the conclusion. But I'm not going to swallow more of this, and I'll save my part for Alypius.[43] For either he'll taste it with me or he'll advise me why I shouldn't touch it." I said, "Navigius has to watch out for sweets with his bad stomach." But he smiled and said, "Clearly such sweets will cure me. For this delicately blended and tasty dish that you have set out of Hymetian honey, as the poet said, is bittersweet and easy to digest.[44] So I willingly swallow the whole thing, as I can, even if my taste is a bit uneasy. For I don't

---

41. The debate presented in the *Answer to the Skeptics* probably began on November 10th. It was interrupted by the discussion of the happy life which began on November 13th and continued on the next two days. See O'Meara's introduction to his translation of the work under the title *Against the Academics*, pp. 24-26, for the probable days of November 386 on which the discussions in the *Answer to the Skeptics*, *The Happy Life* and *Order* take place.

42. In the *Answer to the Skeptics* I, 3, 7, Augustine informs his companions that "it was Cicero's view that a man is happy if he is seeking the truth, even though he is unable to find it." See Cicero, *Hortensius*, fragment 101.

43. In the *Answer to the Skeptics* I, 2, 5 Alypius announces his intention to go to the city; he is absent for the discussion reported in *The Happy Life*. Alypius, like Augustine, was a native of Thagaste, and he will soon become its bishop.

44. See Cicero, *Academic Philosophy* II, 24, 75; *Hortensius*, fragment 89.

see how the conclusion can be rebutted." "Indeed, there is no way that it can be," Trygetius said. "So I'm glad that I have long been an opponent of the Academics. For, by some impulse of nature or, to speak more correctly, of God, I was still very much against them though I didn't know how they were to be refuted."

15. Then Licentius said, "I'm not going to abandon them yet." "So," Trygetius said, "you're going to disagree with us?" And he said, "But aren't you disagreeing with Alypius?" To this I said, "I'm sure that, if Alypius were here, he would yield to this little argument. For he couldn't be so silly as to think that someone is happy if he doesn't have so great a good of the mind that he ardently desires to have, or that they don't want to find the truth, or that someone who isn't happy is wise. For the dish that you're afraid to taste is made from these three ingredients as though from honey, grain and nuts." "Would Alypius abandon the great richness of the Academics and yield to this childish trap? The flood of their richness would either overturn or drag off this short argument." "As if," I said, "we should seek something lengthy, especially for Alypius; for his own body is no mean argument that such small things are strong and quite effective. But you who have chosen to rely on your absent friend's authority,[45] which of these do you reject? That someone isn't happy if he doesn't have what he wants? Or do you deny that they want to find and have the truth? Or do you think that a wise man isn't happy? "Of course," he said smiling sarcastically, "a person is happy if he doesn't have what he wants." But when I ordered that this be written down, he yelled, "I didn't say that." And when I indicated that this too be written down, he admitted, "I said it." For I had insisted once and for all that not a word should escape being written down.[46] Thus I held the young man torn between embarrassment and consistency.

16. While we were egging him on jokingly to eat his portion, so to speak, I saw that the rest were looking on without a smile.

45. Licentius tries to rest his case on the authority of Alypius, but Augustine forces him to take a stand on reason. The theme of authority and reason, or of faith and reason, runs through the early dialogues.
46. This incident seems to indicate that the dialogues really took place and were recorded by a secretary; see *Answer to the Skeptics* I, 1, 4. Also see O'Meara's introduction, pp. 23-32, for the arguments pro and con regarding the historicity of the dialogues.

For they were unaware of this issue and wanted to know what it was that we alone found so amusing.[47] They reminded me of people dining among greedy and boorish guests at a banquet—not a rare occurrence—who either restrain themselves by their good manners or are deterred by modesty from grabbing. Since I was the host and since you taught me[48] that the host plays the role of a great and—to say it all—a true man even in those banquets, I was concerned by the inequality and discrepancy at our table. I smiled at my mother, and she freely ordered that more be brought out as though from her own storeroom because they had less. "Now," she said, "tell us and explain who these Academics are and what they mean." I explained this to her briefly and clearly so that no one would leave uninformed about them. Then she said, "These men have the falling sickness."[49] (That's our common expression for those afflicted with epilepsy.) Then she immediately got up to leave. And so with merriment and laughter we made an end and departed.

3, 17. On the next day, once again after dinner, but a little later than on the day before, the same group of us gathered in the same spot. I said, "You're late in coming to the banquet. I suspect that this isn't because you ate too much yesterday but because you are confident that the courses will be sparse today. So you figured that you shouldn't attack so early what you feel sure you will quickly eat your way through. After all, one should not expect many left-overs when on the day of the feast itself there wasn't much to be found. Perhaps you're right. I myself, like you, don't know what has been prepared for you today. For there is someone else who ceaselessly offers to everyone all feasts, but especially feasts of this sort,[50] though we generally cease to eat because of weakness or satiety or some other concern. Unless I'm mistaken, we piously but firmly agreed yesterday that he remains in men and makes

47. Only Trygetius, Licentius and Alypius had been with Augustine for the discussion in the first book of the *Answer to the Skeptics*; hence, the others are at a loss when the topic of the previous discussion is introduced.
48. Augustine probably refers to Christ, the one teacher.
49. Monica again takes charge, dismisses the skeptics as sick people and brings the discussion to a halt.
50. Once again it is the divine teacher who provides all feasts, but especially the feasts for the mind.

them happy. For, after reason had proven that a person is happy if he has God—and none of you rejected this idea—we asked who you thought has God. If I remember correctly, three opinions were expressed on this. Some of you believed that someone has God if he does what God wants. And others said that someone has God if he lives well. But the rest thought that God is present in those who don't have a spirit that is called unclean.

18. "But it's possible that you have all expressed the very same thought in different words. For, if we consider the first two, everyone who lives a good life does what God wants, and everyone who does what God wants lives a good life. To live a good life is the same as doing what is pleasing to God, or do you think otherwise?" They agreed with me. "The third opinion has to be considered a bit more carefully since a spirit—as I understand it—is usually called unclean in two senses in the ceremony of our sacred mysteries.[51] In the first sense such a spirit enters the soul from outside, confuses the senses, and inflicts a man with a kind of madness. To drive out such an unclean spirit those who preside are said to impose their hands or to exorcize, that is, to drive out by commanding in God's name. In another sense absolutely every unclean soul is called an unclean spirit because it is befouled by vices and errors. And so, my son, since you may have expressed that opinion with a calmer and cleaner spirit, I ask you who you think doesn't have an unclean spirit? Someone who doesn't have a demon by which men are usually made insane, or someone who has cleansed his soul from all vices and sins?" "He who lives a chaste life," he said, "seems to me not to have an unclean spirit." "But whom do you call chaste?" I asked. "Someone who has no sin or only the person who avoids sinful intercourse?" "How can one be chaste," he asked, "if he only avoids sinful intercourse but doesn't restrain himself and stop being defiled by other sins. He is truly chaste who looks to God and directs himself toward God

---

51. This reference to baptism and its rite of exorcism is significant, since it provides some textual evidence against Prosper Alfaric's claim that Augustine was converted in 386 merely to Neoplatonism and only later became Christian. In *L'évolution intellectuelle de saint Augustin* I (Paris 1918), he claimed: "In him the Christian disappeared behind the disciple of Plotinus. If he had died after writing the *Soliloquies*, he would be known as a convinced Neoplatonist, more or less tempted by Christianity."

alone." I wanted these words of the lad written down just as he had said them. "Therefore," I said, "such a person necessarily lives a good life, and he who lives a good life is necessarily such a person, unless you think otherwise." He agreed along with the others. "Therefore," I said, "we are all of the same opinion."

19. "I have another little question for you: Does God want us to seek him?" They said that he did. "I also ask whether we can say that someone who seeks God lives a bad life." "Of course not," they answered. "Answer then this third question: Can an unclean spirit seek God?" Though Navigius hesitated somewhat, they said that it could not. "Therefore, if someone who seeks God does what God wants and lives a good life and doesn't have an unclean spirit, and if someone who seeks God doesn't yet have God, it isn't true that whoever lives a good life or does what God wants or doesn't have an unclean spirit should right away be said to have God." At this point, the rest chuckled at having been trapped by their own admissions, but my mother, who had long been silent, demanded that I loosen and unravel for her with an explanation this knot that I had tied together with the necessity of a conclusion.[52] When I had done this, she said, "No one can come to God unless he seeks God." "Fine," I said, "but someone who is still seeking hasn't yet arrived, and he is already living a good life. Therefore, it isn't true that whoever is living a good life has God." She said, "It seems to me that everyone has God, but that someone who lives a good life has God as a friend and someone who lives a bad life has God as an enemy." "Therefore," I said, "we were wrong yesterday in granting that someone who has God is happy, since everyone has God and yet everyone is not happy." "So," she said, "add 'as a friend.'"

20. "Are we at least agreed that someone who has God as a friend is happy?" Navigius said, "I'd like to agree, but I'm troubled about someone who is still seeking—especially lest you conclude that an Academic is happy, who is the sort of person that in yesterday's conversation was said to have the falling sick-

---

52. Again Monica insists upon an explanation and also introduces the crucial distinction between simply having God and having God as a friend or as an enemy. In doing this she solves the paradox of God's presence, even to the soul that is alienated from God.

ness (in a common, but poor Latin expression, though in my mind one that's quite apt). For I cannot say that God is an enemy to someone who is seeking God. But if it's wrong to say that, God will be friendly, and someone who has God as a friend is happy. Therefore, someone who is seeking will be happy; someone, however, who is seeking doesn't yet have what he wants. Someone, therefore, who doesn't have what he wants will be happy—something all of us yesterday regarded as ridiculous—and as a result we believed that we had dispelled the darkness of the Academics. So now Licentius will win out over us, and like a wise physician he will warn me that I shall pay for those sweets that I so rashly ate without regard for my health."

21. Even my mother laughed, and Trygetius said, "I don't admit right off that God is an enemy to someone toward whom he is not a friend; rather I think there is some middle position." I said to him, "That man in the middle toward whom God is neither a friend nor an enemy—do you admit that he has God in some way?" He hesitated, and my mother said, "It's one thing to have God and another not to be without God." "Which, then, is better," I asked, "to have God or not to be without God?" "As far as I can see," she said, "this is my opinion: Someone who lives a good life has God, but he has God as a friend; someone who lives a bad life has God as an enemy; and someone who still seeks and hasn't found doesn't have God as a friend or as an enemy, but isn't without God." "Is this what the rest of you think?" I asked. They said that it was. "Then tell me, please, do you think that God is a friend to a man he favors?" They granted that he is. "But doesn't God," I said, "favor a man who is seeking him?" They answered that he does. "Therefore, someone who is seeking God has God as a friend, and everyone who has God as a friend is happy. Hence, someone who is still seeking is happy, even though someone who is still seeking doesn't have what he wants. And so, a person who doesn't have what he wants will be happy." "Certainly," my mother said, "I don't think that someone who doesn't have what he wants is happy." "Hence," I said, "not everyone who has God as a friend is happy." "If reason forces us to this," she said, "I cannot deny it." "So," I said, "the situation will be that everyone who has already found God both has God as a friend and is happy. But whoever

separates himself from God by vices and sins isn't only unhappy but also doesn't live with God as his friend."

22. Everyone was satisfied with this, and I said, "Fine, but I'm still afraid that what we granted earlier may change your mind, namely, that whoever isn't happy is unhappy. The result will be that a man is unhappy if he [has God as a friend, because—as we said—he still seeks God and thus isn't yet happy.][53] 'Or shall we,' as Tully said, 'call the lords of many estates in the land wealthy and call the possessors of all the virtues poor?'[54] See whether it isn't true that, as every needy man is unhappy, every unhappy man is needy. For then it will be true that unhappiness is the same as neediness—and you have seen that I approved this idea when it was expressed. But this is a long question to look into today; so I hope that it will be no trouble for you to gather around this table again tomorrow." All said that they would be happy to do so, and we got up to leave.

4, 23. The morning of the third day of our discussion scattered the clouds which had forced us into the baths and gave us sunny afternoon weather. So we decided to go down to the nearby fields, and when we were all seated where it seemed comfortable, the rest of the conversation continued. "I now have in my possession almost everything that I wanted you to grant me as I was questioning you. So today—to divide up our banquet over several days—I think that there will be little or nothing left that you have to answer. For my mother said that unhappiness was nothing other than neediness, and we all agreed that those who are in need are unhappy. But there is still some question as to whether all the unhappy are also needy, and we were unable to answer this yesterday. If reason proves that this is so, we shall have discovered precisely who is happy. For it will be someone who isn't needy. For everyone who isn't unhappy is happy. Therefore, he who is without need is happy, if we have established that unhappiness is the same thing as what we call neediness."

---

53. Augustine mentions this lacuna in *Revisions* I, 2. The Migne edition fills in the lacuna with the text in brackets.
54. This reference is perhaps to *Hortensius*.

24. "But look," Trygetius said, "can't we conclude that everyone who isn't needy is happy from the fact that everyone who is needy is clearly unhappy? For I recall our having granted that there is no middle position between unhappy and happy." I said, "Do you think that there is a middle position between dead and alive? Isn't every human being either alive or dead?" "I admit," he said, "that there is no middle position here, but what's the point?" "The point," I said, "is that I believe that you admit that everyone buried a year ago is dead." He agreed. "But is everyone who wasn't buried a year ago living?" He said, "That doesn't follow." "Therefore," I said, "it doesn't follow that, if everyone who is needy is unhappy, everyone who isn't needy is happy, even though no middle position can be found between unhappy and happy or between living and dead."

25. Some of them grasped this point a bit more slowly while I explained it and rephrased it in words better suited to their minds. Then I said, "Therefore, no one doubts that everyone in need is unhappy, and the bodily needs of the wise don't shake our position. For the mind itself, in which is found the happy life, doesn't need these things.[55] The mind itself is perfect, and nothing perfect needs anything. It will take what seems necessary for the body if it is available, and if it isn't, the lack of such things won't crush it. For every wise person is brave, and no one who is brave fears anything. Therefore, a wise person doesn't fear either death or the pains of the body, and it is to dispel, avoid, or postpone these that he has need of such things as he might lack. The wise person, nonetheless, continues to use them well if they are available. For that verse contains a great

---

55. See *Revisions* I, 2. Augustine remarks that he was displeased because he said "that the happy life resided only in the mind of a wise person during his own lifetime, in whatever state his body might be." That is, Augustine admits that when he wrote *The Happy Life* he thought that the wise person even in this life enjoyed a happiness than which no greater could be hoped for hereafter and that he thought of this happiness as purely a matter of the mind (*animus*) and not of the body. For the Stoic origin of this doctrine, see *Stoicorum Veterum Fragmenta* III, 151, fragment 572.

O'Connell notes that in *The Happy Life* 22-23 Augustine employs key Stoic notions, such as independence of exterior goods of fortune, "measure in all things," and the limitation of desires to what one has. He cites Cicero three times with approval and appeals to him at crucial points in the argument. See O'Connell, *Early Theory* 194-195.

deal of truth: 'For it is foolish to endure what you can avoid.'[56] Thus, a wise person will avoid death and pain as much as he can and as much as is proper. For, if he could have avoided them, he would be unhappy not because such things befell him but because he could have avoided them and didn't—a sure sign of folly. Thus someone who doesn't avoid them will be unhappy not by reason of his suffering these things but by reason of his folly. If, however, he was unable to avoid them, though he was acting with carefulness and decency, then those things won't make him unhappy when they descend upon him. For the saying of the same comic poet is no less true: 'Since what you want cannot be, want what is in your power.'[57] How will he be unhappy if nothing happens against his will, since he cannot want what he sees he cannot have? For he wants things that are most certain, that is, so that he does whatever he does only out of some command of virtue and the divine law of wisdom, which can never be taken from him.

26. "Now let's see whether everyone who is unhappy is in need. A difficulty in granting this claim comes from the fact that this life is still difficult for many people who have a great abundance of the goods of fortune, even though everything is so easy for them that whatever they desire is immediately at hand. Still, let's imagine someone such as Tully claims Orata to have been.[58] For who would readily claim that Orata, a man with great wealth, charm, and culture, suffered need? He lacked nothing as regards pleasure, charm, or good and sound health. For he had all the rich estates and pleasant friends that he could want, and he used all his possessions well for the health of the body, and—to be brief—everything he undertook and everything he desired turned out well. Perhaps one of you will say that he wanted to have more

---

56. Terence, *The Eunuch* 761.
57. Terence, *Andria* 305; see *The Trinity* XIII, 7,10, where Augustine says, "This is the whole happiness of proud mortals—whether it is something we should laugh at or rather pity—who boast that they live as they want. They willingly bear in patience what they do not want to happen to them. This they say is the advice of Terence, 'Since what you want cannot be, want what is in your power.' Who denies that this is good advice? But it is advice given to an unhappy man lest he become more wretched."
58. See Cicero, *Hortensius*, fragment 76.

than he had. We don't know this. But let's suppose—as will suffice for our investigation—that he didn't desire more than he had. Do you think that he was in need?" "Even if I should concede," said Licentius, "that he didn't desire more, though I don't know how I can admit this in the case of a someone who isn't wise, he still feared—for he wasn't, it is said, unintelligent—that all these possessions might be taken away from him in one adverse blow. For it isn't hard to understand that all such things—as magnificent as they are—are subject to fortune." Then with a smile I said, "You see, Licentius, this most fortunate of men was kept from the happy life by the quality of his intelligence. The sharper he was, the more clearly he saw that he could lose everything; and he was shattered by this fear. The old proverb put it well enough, 'A bad man is clever to his own disadvantage.'"[59]

27. Licentius and the rest laughed, and I said, "Still, let's look at that example more closely. For, although he was in fear, he wasn't in need. Hence, our question remains. To be in need consists in not having, not in the fear of losing what you have. But he was unhappy because he was in fear, even though he wasn't in need. Therefore, not everyone who is unhappy is needy." My mother, whose position I was defending, gave her approval along with the rest, though she was still a bit hesitant. Then she said, "I still don't know and clearly grasp how unhappiness can be separated from neediness or neediness from unhappiness. For that person who was rich and wealthy and, as you say, desired nothing more was still in need of wisdom, since he feared losing what he had. Are we, then, going to say that someone is needy if he lacks money and not needy if he lacks wisdom?"[60] All exclaimed in wonder, and I was myself more than a little pleased, especially because it was my mother who stated what I had prepared to set before them at the end as something great drawn from the books of the philosophers. I said, "Do you see how different it is to have all sorts of learning and to have one's mind set upon God? For where but from that source did she get these words we admire so

---

59. This is a proverb of uncertain origin.
60. Once again Monica makes the crucial distinction and speaks of the importance of wisdom. She whose simple faith had led Augustine to seek a more sophisticated wisdom in Manicheanism is now portrayed as a lover of wisdom.

much?" Licentius then joyfully exclaimed, "Indeed nothing more
true, nothing more divine could be said. For there is no greater or
more wretched need than to need wisdom, and one who doesn't
stand in need of wisdom cannot be in need of anything at all."

28. "Then, neediness of the mind," I said, "is simply folly. For
folly is the opposite of wisdom, and it's just as much the opposite
as death is to life and as the happy life is to unhappiness, that
is, without anything in the middle. For, as everyone not happy
is unhappy and as everyone not dead is living, so it's clear that
everyone not foolish is wise. Hence, you can see now that Sergius
Orata was unhappy not so much because he feared to lose his gifts
of fortune but because he was foolish. Thus he would be even
more unhappy if he hadn't feared at all for these wavering and
unstable things, which he considered goods. For he would owe
his security not to courageous vigilance but to mental dullness,
and the unhappy man would be plunged into deeper folly. But, if
everyone who lacks wisdom suffers great need and if everyone
possessing wisdom needs nothing, it follows that folly is neediness. As every fool is unhappy, so everyone unhappy is a fool.
Therefore, as all neediness is unhappiness, so all unhappiness is
shown to be neediness."

29. Trygetius said that he hadn't quite grasped this conclusion, and so I said, "What has reason led us to agree upon?" He
answered, "That someone is in need if he doesn't have wisdom."
"What is it, then," I said, "to be in need?" He said, "Not to have
wisdom." "What is it," I said, "not to have wisdom?" He had no
answer; so I said, "Isn't it to have folly?" "It is," he said. "Therefore, to have need is simply to have folly; hence, it must be that
we merely call neediness by another name when we say folly,
though I don't know how we can say, 'He has need' or 'He has
folly.' It's just like saying that some place lacking light has darkness, which is merely not having light. For darkness doesn't really
come and go; rather, to lack light is itself to be dark, just as to lack
clothing is to be naked. For when clothing approaches, nakedness
does not take off like something real and movable. Thus we say
that someone has need in the same way we say that someone has
nakedness. Neediness is a word for not having. Hence, to explain
what I want as best I can, we say, 'He has need,' just as we say,

'He doesn't have having.' Therefore, if we have shown that folly itself is true and certain neediness, see whether or not the question that we raised has been answered. For we were in doubt whether in mentioning unhappiness we were simply speaking of neediness. But we have proven that folly is correctly called neediness. Therefore, as every fool is unhappy, and every unhappy person is foolish, so it is necessary that we admit not only that everyone in need is unhappy but also that everyone who is unhappy is in need. But, if from the premises that every fool is unhappy and every unhappy man is foolish, we conclude that folly is unhappiness, why don't we conclude from the premises—that whoever is in need is unhappy and that whoever is unhappy is in need—that unhappiness is nothing other than neediness?"

30. Everyone admitted that it was so, and then I said, "The next thing is to see who isn't in need. For that person will be both wise and happy. Folly, however, is neediness and the name for neediness. This word usually indicates a kind of barrenness and deprivation. Look more deeply, please, and note the great care with which the ancients created either all or, clearly, at least some words, especially for those things that we need to know most of all. For you admit that every fool is in need and that everyone in need is a fool. I believe that you also admit that a foolish mind is full of defects and that all defects of the mind are included under the single word 'folly.' On the first day of our discussion, we had said that wickedness (*nequitia*) was so called from the fact that it isn't anything (*nec quicquam*) and that its opposite was called fruitfulness (*frugalitas*) from fruit (*frux*).[61] Hence, in these two opposites, that is, in fruitfulness and wickedness, two things seem to stand out, being and non-being. But what are we to think is the opposite of neediness, which is the subject of our investigation?" They hesitated, but then Trygetius said, "If I say wealth, I see that its opposite is poverty." "That's indeed close," I said, "for poverty and neediness are usually taken to be one and the same thing. Yet we should find another word so that the better side isn't lacking a term. As the other side has the names poverty and neediness, this side should have more than the name wealth. For nothing

---

61. See above, 2, 8.

would be more ridiculous than that there be a need of a term as an opposite of neediness." Licentius said, "Plenitude, if one can use that expression, seems to me to be correctly opposed to neediness."

31. "Later," I said, "we shall perhaps look more closely at the word; in seeking the truth that shouldn't be our main concern. Though Sallust, who most carefully weighed his words, opposed 'opulence' to 'neediness,' I'll still accept 'plenitude.'[62] For here we'll be free from fear of grammarians and shouldn't be afraid that we'll be punished by them for carelessly using words, when they have given us their estate to use."[63] They smiled, and I said, "I'm determined to regard your minds as oracles of sorts, while you are intent upon God, and so let's see what this word means. For I think that no word is better suited to the truth. Plenitude and neediness, then, are opposites, and here too, as in the case of wickedness and fruitfulness, that pair also shows up, namely, being and non-being. If neediness is folly itself, then plenitude will be wisdom. Not without reason have many said that fruitfulness is the mother of all virtues. And in agreement with them, Tully said in his popular discourse, 'Let anyone hold what he wants, but I still judge that fruitfulness, that is, moderation and temperance, is the greatest virtue.'[64] He spoke most learnedly and with great propriety. For he had in mind fruit, that is, what we called being, whose opposite is non-being. But on account of the common usage by which frugality (*frugalitas*) is usually regarded as stinginess, he explained what he meant by the next two words which he added, namely, moderation and temperance. So let us look more carefully at these two words.

32. "Moderation is, of course, derived from limit (*modus*) and temperance from harmonious balance (*temperies*). Where there is limit and balance, there is neither too much nor too little. This, then, is the plenitude that we have opposed to neediness much more correctly than if we had used 'abundance.' For in abundance there is understood an overflowing and a gushing forth of some-

---

62. Sallust, *Catiline's Conspiracy* 52, 22.
63. In *Order* I, 2, 5, Augustine says that he and his friends had withdrawn "to the villa of our close friend, Verecundus." From this passage we learn that Verecundus was a professor of grammar.
64. Cicero, *Tusculan Disputations* III, 8, 16.

thing excessively rich. And when this happens beyond what is enough, a limit is wanting even there, and what is excessive lacks a limit. Hence, need is no stranger to superfluity, but both too much and too little are strangers to limit. If you analyze richness, you will find that it holds a just limit. For richness (*opulentia*) is derived from riches (*ops*). How can what is too much enrich, since it's often less advantageous than too little? Hence, whatever is too much or too little, because it lacks limit, is subject to need. The limit of the mind, then, is wisdom. For wisdom is admittedly the opposite of folly, and folly is neediness; however, plenitude is the opposite of neediness. Hence, wisdom is plenitude. But in plenitude there is limit; the mind's limit is wisdom. Thus that famous saying is deservedly often cited: 'This first of all is useful in life: Nothing to excess.'[65]

33. "At the beginning of today's discussion, however, we said that, if we discover that unhappiness is simply neediness, we would admit that a man who needs nothing is happy.[66] And we have made that discovery. Therefore, to be happy is simply not to be needy, that is, to be wise. But, if you ask what wisdom is, reason has—to the extent that it could here and now—opened up and uncovered this as well. For it is simply the limit of the mind, that is, that by which the mind holds itself in balance so that it doesn't run off into excesses and isn't held back below the full mark. A mind runs off into luxuries, positions of power, pride, and that sort of thing, by which the minds of the immoderate and unhappy think that they are acquiring joy and power. A mind is held back by filth, fear, depression, lust and by whatever it is by which men admit that they are unhappy. But let the mind discover and gaze upon wisdom, and—to use this lad's expression[67]—let it direct itself toward wisdom and, undisturbed by any inanity, not turn to the deception of images. For, once it embraces the weight of such things, the mind usually falls from God and sinks down. If

---

65. Terence, *Andria* 61.
66. See above 4, 23.
67. See above 3, 18. At this point one suddenly sees that the Stoic virtues of moderation and temperance, with an emphasis on limit and balance, are transformed into extra-mental hypostases. That is, Augustine is showing that the values of Stoicism have to be assumed into a Plotinian metaphysics. On this point, see O'Connell, *Early Theory* 94-95.

the mind gazes upon wisdom, it has no fear of immoderation and, hence, of neediness or of unhappiness. Whoever is happy has his limit, that is, wisdom.

34. "What should we call wisdom if not that wisdom which is God's? We have it on the authority of God himself that the Son of God is God's wisdom,[68] and the Son of God is surely God. Therefore, whoever is happy has God. We had all agreed on this when we began this banquet. But what do you think wisdom is, if not the truth? For scripture also says, *I am the truth* (Jn 14:6). In order that he might be the truth, he comes to be through some highest limit, from which he proceeds and to which he turns back, when he is perfect.[69] No other limit is placed upon the highest limit. For, if the highest limit is a limit through the highest limit, it is a limit through itself. But it is also necessary that the highest limit be a true limit. Therefore, as truth is born from the limit, so the limit is known through the truth. The truth, then, has never been without the limit, nor has the limit been without truth. Who is the Son of God? Scripture says, *The truth*. Who is it that has no father? Who else but the highest limit? Whoever shall have come to the highest limit through the truth is happy. For minds to have God is precisely this: To enjoy God. Though God has all other things, they don't have God.

35. "A certain warning which works with us so that we remember God, so that we seek him, so that we thirst for him with no lack of thirst, flows from the very fountain of truth to us. That hidden sun pours forth this radiance for our inner eyes.[70] His is every truth we speak, even when with less healthy or suddenly opened eyes we're still afraid to turn boldly and gaze upon the whole truth, and this too is clearly God, perfect and without any lessening of perfection. For there everything is whole and perfect and at the same time omnipotent God. But as long as we're seeking and our thirst isn't yet quenched by the fountain itself and—to use the previous word—by plenitude, we admit that we haven't yet arrived at our limit. Thus, even though God is now helping us, we aren't yet wise

---

68. See 1 Cor 1:24; see also *Answer to the Skeptics* II, 1, 1.
69. See Plotinus, *Ennead* I, 2, 2; 8, 2, for the philosophical background in terms of which Augustine is articulating the procession of the Son from the Father.
70. See *Soliloquies* I, 8, 15; *The Teacher* 11, 38; *The City of God* X, 2.

and happy. That, then, is full satiety of minds, namely, the happy life, to know piously and perfectly that by which you are led into the truth, that truth which you enjoy, and that through which you are joined to the highest limit.[71] These three reveal one God and one substance—God for those who understand—with the exclusion of the vanities of various superstitions." My mother recognized these words, which were fixed deep in her memory, and, as though awakening into her faith, uttered joyously that verse of our priest: "Cherish us as we pray, O Trinity,"[72] and added, "This is without doubt the happy life, and that life is perfect toward which we can, we must presume, be quickly brought through solid faith, lively hope, and burning love."

36. "Therefore, since the limit itself," I said, "also warns us to divide our banquet over an interval of days, I offer all the thanks I can to the highest and true God, the Father, to the Lord, the deliverer of souls, and finally to you, my guests, who have in unity of heart loaded me with gifts. For you have contributed so much to our conversation that I have to admit that I've been brought to satiety by my guests." Then, as everyone was joyously praising God, Trygetius said, "How I wish that you would feed us this way every day." "You must," I said, "everywhere preserve and everywhere love that limit, if you have at heart our return to God." With these words our discussion ended, and we went off.

---

71. Here we have Augustine's first attempt to present an understanding of the mystery of the Trinity. The Father is the limit (*modus*); the Son is the truth (*veritas*) that is born of the limit and that makes the limit known; the Spirit is the warning (*admonitio*) by which we are brought to the truth. He insists upon the unity of substance among the three and excludes unambiguously any subordination of the Son or the Spirit to the Father, despite his use of Neoplatonic terms and a Neoplatonic framework. See O'Connell, *Early Theory* 264-265.
72. Augustine cites Ambrose's hymn, *Deus Creator Omnium* (2, 32), which is still found in the modern breviary. If the thesis of *The Happy Life* is that happiness is found only in God, Monica's exclamation points out how happiness is to be obtained: through prayer. See O'Connell, *Early Theory* 77.

Faith in the Unseen

Translation by Michael G. Campbell, O.S.A.
Introduction and notes
by Michael Fiedrowicz

Introduction

1. Authenticity and Date

Since neither Augustine in the *Revisions* nor Possidius in the *Indiculus* mentions this work, Erasmus cast doubt on its authenticity in the edition of Augustine's works that he published in 1528.[1] In his view, Hugh of St. Victor composed it in the twelfth century by putting together statements of Augustine, especially from his letters. The editors of the critical Louvain edition (1577) adopted this position, as did Robert Bellarmine in his catalogue of Christian authors, *De scriptoribus ecclesiasticis* (1613). But soon thereafter scholars became convinced that Augustine was the author.

An important argument in favor of authenticity is Augustine's letter to his friend Darius, in which, along with other books, he mentions this work under the title *De fide rerum quae non videntur (liber).*[2]

Many editors departed from the title given in all the manuscripts, *De fide rerum invisibilium (liber)*, and adopted instead the title attested by Augustine himself.[3]

The work must have been composed after 399. In sections 4, 7 and 7, 10 there are references to the destruction of the statues of the gods and of temples that occurred in North Africa after the promulgation of an antipagan law by Emperor Honorius in 399. It is more difficult to determine the *terminus ante quem*. Augustine's

---

1. See *Quartus tomus omnium operum divi Aurelii Augustini* (Basel 1528) 695.
2. Letter 231, 7.
3. See, for example, the Maurist edition in PL 40, 171.

letter 231 was composed in 429/30. Material parallels to books 17
and 18 of *The City of God* suggest a date between 420 and 425.[4]

2. Literary Genre and Structure

Scholars disagree on the literary classification of *Faith in the
Unseen*. Some consider it to be an apologetical treatise (*liber*),
and indeed the logical sequence of arguments, the lack of spon-
taneity, and the scarcity of personal touches seem to confirm this
characterization.[5] The Maurists were the first to classify the work
as a *tractatus popularis*, that is, an address (*sermo*) to believers,
either catechumens or newly baptized, that sought to strengthen
them in their faith so that they might also be able to defend it
against attacks by nonbelievers.[6]

The address combines elements of apologetic and exhortation. The primary intention is an appeal (*suasio*) for faith, but the
strengthening of faith is done by refuting opponents' arguments
and by demonstrating the reasonableness and credibility of faith
itself.

The classification of the work as an exhortatory address (*oratio
suasoria*) is confirmed by a rhetorical analysis of the introduction,
the conclusion, and the speech of the personified Church in the
body of the work.

The structure of the work is simple and clear:

Introduction:
    Presentation of the subject and of the method of treatment
       (1, 1)
Main section:
    Refutation of criticisms of religious faith; demonstration
    of the necessity of faith (1, 2-3, 4)

---

4. See M. P. J. van den Hout, ed., "Praefatio," in Augustine, *De fide rerum invisibilium*,
CCL XLVI, lxi.
5. According to M. F. McDonald, *Saint Augustine's De fide rerum quae non videntur. A
Critical Text and Translation with Introduction and Commentary* (Washington 1950)
51-57.
6. See N. Cipriani, "De fide rerum quae non videntur," in *De vera religione; De utilitate
credendi; De fide rerum quae non videntur* (Rome 1994) 95-109.

Evidences for the credibility of the Catholic faith
    (3, 5-7, 10)
Conclusion:
    An appeal to the faithful to nourish their faith and allow it to
grow (8, 11)

3. The Line of Argument

The "unseen things" (*rerum invisibilium*) alluded to in the title
as an object of faith are not only realities that are by their nature
invisible, such as the divine Trinity. They also include all the
events of salvation history, whether past, such as the incarnation,
resurrection, and ascension of Christ, or eschatological, such as the
resurrection of the dead and the universal judgment. The problem
is this: May one believe in past or future events, of which one has
neither direct experience nor rational proof? More concretely:
Does what the Christian faith teaches have credibility? The answer
to both questions forms the basic content of *Faith in the Unseen*.

a) The Necessity of Religious Faith

The point of departure of the argument is the refusal of the
opponents of faith to accept realities of which they have no sense
experience.[7] With his reference to human will-acts and thoughts,
which can be grasped only intellectually, Augustine makes a first
breach in his opponents' wall of defense. In a further step, he uses
the example of feelings of friendship to prove that no immediate
knowledge is possible here but only a belief based on outward
signs: deeds, gestures, words. Faith can therefore be defined as
a knowledge that is based not on direct sense experience nor on
awareness of the self but on outward signs.[8]

In this analysis of faith, as in other works,[9] Augustine's primary
purpose is to elucidate the epistemological value of faith. As he had
already done in *The Advantage of Believing*, here too he emphasizes
the indispensable need of faith in human social life: "If trust of this

---

7. *Faith in the Unseen* 1, 1.
8. Ibid. 1, 2-2, 3.
9. See *Confessions* VI, 5, 7; *The Advantage of Believing* 11, 25; *The Trinity* IX, 1.

kind were to disappear from human affairs, how could anyone escape being aware of the confusion and appalling upheaval which would follow? Since the love of which we speak is unseen, who then could enjoy the mutual love of another?"[10] Without the invisible trust one places in his fellow human beings, his friends, his relatives, the social life of humankind would become hopelessly confused. This argument now forms the basis for demonstrating the reasonableness of faith in the religious sphere as well.

Augustine is convinced that faith in things divine is even more necessary because, if one rejects this faith, "not merely would certain human friendships suffer profanations, but it would extend even to the most supreme form of religion itself, with the direst possible consequences."[11] This argument is convincing, of course, only in the light of faith itself. Those who do not yet believe in a life after death will hardly be moved by the consequences against which Augustine warns those who refuse to believe.

This last point makes it clear that Augustine has chiefly in mind a circle of readers within the Church. In his apologetical treatise, *The Advantage of Believing*, he argued that faith is even more important in the religious sphere than in daily life because it is so difficult to know divine truths. Here, in *Faith in the Unseen*, he uses the practical argument from the greater risk that the refusal of faith entails in the religious sphere.

b) The Credibility of the Christian Faith

After this general proof of the necessity of religious faith, Augustine now explains the credibility of the Christian faith in particular.[12] His opponent has meanwhile changed his position: he no longer rejects faith in principle but accepts faith in the unseen as legitimate on the basis of certain evidences. But he now demands such evidences of credibility for the Christian faith. Augustine answers: "Those people who allege that our faith in Christ lacks any proof are greatly mistaken."[13]

---

10. *Faith in the Unseen* 2, 4.
11. Ibid. 3, 4.
12. Ibid. 3, 5-7, 10.
13. Ibid. 3, 5.

He immediately turns his opponent's attention to the decisive point: "You, then, who think that no visible proofs exist which would enable you to believe in Christ, should pay attention to the things you can actually see."[14] In his argument Augustine is turning back to the proof from evidence in ancient rhetoric. According to Quintilian's definition, an *indicium* is "something by means of which one becomes aware of something else, just as, for example, one becomes aware of a murder through the presence of blood."[15] What evidences or signs can one adduce by means of which the credibility of the content of Christian faith can be known? Augustine points first of all to the fulfillment of Old Testament prophecies concerning the Church and then to the astonishing spread of Christianity throughout the world.

If the Old Testament promises of the conversion of the nations to Christ and to the only God have been fulfilled in the Church, then this visible Church is in turn a sign of things that are presently unseen. But just as the Church was shown forth in the scriptures, so these unseen things may now belong either to the past (the life of Christ, for example) or to the future (the universal judgment).[16] "Why is it then that we refuse to believe the first and the last things, which we do not see, although we have as witnesses of both the things midway between them, which we do see? I am referring to those prophetic writings in which we either hear or read how these first, middle and last things were foretold before they came to pass."[17] The evidence of present fulfillment guarantees the credibility also of biblical statements for which this evidence does not presently exist: "You did not see what was foretold and brought to pass regarding the human birth of Christ: *Behold, a virgin shall conceive and bear a son* (Mt 1:23; Is 7:14), yet what you can see is how the promise made to Abraham has been fulfilled: *In your offspring all the nations of the earth shall be blessed* (Gn 22:18)."[18]

---

14. Ibid.
15. Quintilian, *Institutio oratoria* 5, 9, 8.
16. *Faith in the Unseen* 5, 8.
17. Ibid.
18. Ibid. 4, 7.

With superb rhetoric Augustine develops this argument in a rather lengthy passage in which he places a hymn-like speech in the mouth of the personified Church:[19] With a motherly love she implores nonbelievers to attend to the signs that make the Christian faith credible: "Does it appear absurd and inconsequential to you, and the divine testimony of little or no worth at all in your estimation, that the whole human race flocks to the name of a single crucified man?"[20]

But the apologetical value of the argument from prophecy seemed to be challenged by two objections. The first was: Were the prophecies about the Church possibly only a Christian interpolation in the Old Testament texts, in order to give its religion a higher authority? Augustine answers by pointing out that these promises are also found in the manuscripts of the Jews, who were to be seen as enemies of Christians. For this very reason they could be regarded as credible witnesses. In addition, the scattering of the Jews meant that the biblical prophecies confirming the Christian claim were also in universal circulation and could convince nonbelievers.[21]

There was, however, another more serious objection. If the Old Testament really prophesied so much with utter clarity about the Church, why did the Jews not understand these prophecies? Augustine skillfully counters with the argument that even the blindness of the Jews was foretold by the prophets as a just punishment of their guilt.[22] Despite all this, the question arises of what persuasive power the argument from prophecy had for a non-Christian readership. As a matter of fact, in his controversy with Faustus the Manichean, Augustine expressly took the position that the fulfillment of many biblical prophecies, especially about the Church, was so evident that it could convince even nonbelievers.[23] Nevertheless in the present work he seems to acknowledge the limited apologetical value of this argument,

---

19. Ibid. 3, 5-4, 7.
20. Ibid. 4, 7.
21. Ibid. 6, 9. On this Augustinian topos see B. Blumenkranz, *Die Judenpredigt Augustins* (Paris: Études Augustiniennes, 1973) 175-178.
22. *Faith in the Unseen* 6, 9.
23. See *Answer to Faustus* 13, 1-14.

since he now passes on to a different kind of argument: "Even were we to suppose that no prior prophetic witnesses existed pertaining to Christ and the Church, what person would not be immediately impelled to believe that the divine splendor had indeed burst forth upon humanity, when he sees how false gods are now abandoned and their images smashed, their temples destroyed or put to another use, and the empty rituals for so long part of human habit discontinued, while the one true God is invoked by the whole human race?"[24] Instead of arguing from a typological interpretation of biblical texts Augustine is here arguing from an objective fact that could be empirically verified even by non-Christians.

Through further arguments Augustine attempts to make it plausible that this undeniable spread of Christianity was due ultimately to a divine intervention. This spread was due to a man whom others mocked, scourged, crucified, and killed; uneducated fishermen and tax collectors proclaimed his message throughout the world and attested to its truth by their deaths; human beings of every age and social class believed the message; all the sects and heresies try to win authority for themselves by using the name of Christ. "How could that crucified one possibly have accomplished so much, if not for the fact that God had assumed human nature?"[25] As Augustine finishes his line of thought, he notches his argument up a degree by pointing out that all these facts are not only convincing in themselves but were in addition foretold by the prophets.

In his conclusion Augustine calls upon his primary addressees—both Christians who have long believed and those who have only recently become believers—to strengthen and deepen their faith and not to let themselves be deceived by anyone outside the Church (pagans, Jews, heretics) or within it (bad Christians).[26]

---

24. *Faith in the Unseen* 7, 10.
25. Ibid.
26. Ibid. 8, 11.

4. The Importance of the Work

Although *Faith in the Unseen*, by reason of its brevity, belongs among Augustine's minor works, it is marked by stylistic elegance, clarity of composition, lucid presentation of ideas, and beauty of expression. The rigorous refutation of a crass empiricism that accepts sense experience as the sole form of knowledge and the rational explanation of another way of knowing realities not directly and empirically verifiable give Augustine's plea for "faith in the unseen" an abiding topicality.

Faith in the Unseen

1, 1. There is a class of people who maintain that the Christian religion should be despised rather than embraced, because what it presents is not something tangible but something that demands faith in matters which lie beyond human vision.[1] In our efforts to refute such people, who consider themselves wise by refusing to believe what they cannot see, even if we are unable to demonstrate visibly the divine truths which we believe, we are nonetheless in a position to demonstrate that the human mind is duty-bound to believe those things which cannot be seen.

In the first place, those people stand rebuked who in their folly believe themselves answerable to what fleshly eyes alone can see and consequently maintain that they are not bound to believe what they cannot see. Yet, in truth, many are the things which they not only believe, and indeed know to be true, but which they cannot see with eyes of that sort. Take this human mind of ours: it is the repository for such an immense number of things, a faculty whose nature remains unseen, to put it simply. Yet that very trust itself by which we believe, the act of thinking through which we know whether we believe or disbelieve something, which is far removed from the sight of those eyes—what else is so resplendent, so clear, and so certain before the interior gaze of our minds than this? How is it, therefore, that what we cannot see with our bodily eyes we are not bound to believe when, without any hesitation and without the assistance of our bodily eyes, we are able to see immediately whether we believe or not?

---

1. See *True Religion* 3, 3.

65

2. "But," they retort, "we have no need to see with the eyes of our body what is in the soul, since we can do that with our mind. You people assert that there are things we should believe, yet you are unable to let us see externally that we may verify them through the evidence of our bodily eyes, nor are such things to be found in our minds so that we may catch sight of them through reflection."

This is the way they argue, as if a person were only bound to believe once he was able to see for himself the object of his belief. Consequently, we must believe in many things pertaining to the temporal realm which we cannot see, so that we may also deserve to see those eternal things which we presently believe in.

But whoever you are,[2] you who refuse to believe what you cannot see: with the evidence of your bodily eyes you can assuredly see physical bodies all around you. With your mind you can also see the inclinations of your will and your thoughts. Tell me then, I beg you, with what manner of vision do you observe the will of a friend in your regard? To actually see the will of any person is beyond the possibilities of the bodily eye. Or is it possible for you to glimpse with your mind what takes place in another person's mind? And if it is the case that you fail to see this, how can you possibly return mutual friendship if you refuse to believe what you cannot see? Or will you perhaps answer that you are indeed able to see the will of someone else manifested through his behavior? Therefore, because of the actions you are about to witness and the words you are going to hear, you intend to believe the intentions of a friend's will in your regard, something which it is impossible to see or hear. For the will we are referring to possesses neither color nor shape so as to be visible, nor has it sound or melody by which it can reach our ears, neither is it your own will of which you are conscious in your heart. The fact remains that what you cannot see or hear or glimpse within yourself you nevertheless believe, lest your life be totally devoid of that friendship and the affection shown you by your friend remain unacknowledged on your part.[3]

---

2. The continual use of direct address shows that this work belongs to the genre of discourse.

3. On Augustine's ideal of friendship see J. T. Lienhard, "Friendship, Friends," in A. D. Fitzgerald, ed., *Augustine Through the Ages* (Grand Rapids: Eerdmans, 1999) 372-373.

So, what about that statement of yours that you should not believe anything unless you see it either externally through the body or internally by the heart? For the truth is that from your heart you trust a heart other than your own and are prepared to believe what you are unable to see either with the eye of your flesh or with that of the mind. With your body you can see the face of a friend, with your mind you can see your own trust, but the trust of your friend cannot be the object of your love if no such mutual trust is found in you, a trust which enables you to believe something you cannot actually see in your friend. However, it is possible for a person to deceive by feigning goodwill and concealing his evil intentions; or, if the intention is not to harm, yet in the hope of gaining some advantage from you he may act deceitfully because he is lacking in love.

3. Yet you insist that you keep faith in your friend, whose heart you cannot see, because you have discovered his worth in time of trial and are aware how he feels towards you, since he refused to abandon you when you were in dire straits. Do you really think, therefore, that we should hope for adversity in order to prove the affection of our friends? And is no one to rest content in the certainty of his friends unless he has first experienced misery through adverse circumstances? In other words, is he not to enjoy the proven friendship of another without first passing through the crucible of suffering and fear? And, in the act of acquiring true friends, how can happiness be desired rather than feared, when happiness is a state which unhappiness alone can prove? Yet the truth of the matter is that in good times we can also have a friend, while bad times only serve to make that friendship even more assured.

2, 3. But, unless you believed in a friend, you would not entrust yourself to him in time of danger so as to prove the worth of his friendship. And so for this reason, when you do entrust yourself to a friend in order to prove his friendship, you are actually putting your faith in him before you have proof that he is your friend. For it remains true that if we are not to believe what we cannot see, yet, at those times when the dispositions of our friends remain somewhat uncertain and we do give them our trust, then, when we eventually ascertain proof of their intentions in adverse circumstances, it still comes down to a matter of believing rather than seeing their goodwill towards us. Unless, perhaps, the degree of trust is such that, through what we may not inappropriately refer to as a kind of eyes that it has, we judge ourselves to see the friendship we believe in when normally we ought to believe what we cannot see.

4. If trust of this kind were to disappear from human affairs, who would not be aware of the confusion and appalling upheaval which would follow? Since the love of which we speak is unseen, who then could enjoy the mutual love of another, if I do not feel bound to believe what I cannot see? Friendship as a whole would therefore disappear, because its essence is mutual love.[4] Who could ever receive anything from another if no visible, credible proof had first been given? Indeed, were friendship to disappear, there would be no way of preserving spiritually those bonds which exist between married couples, families and relatives, for the harmony characteristic of these relationships has its basis in friendship. It would therefore be impossible for a husband to show mutual love to his wife since, unable to see the love for himself, he would not believe she loved him. Likewise, they would cherish no desire to have children because they would not believe that they would return their love. If it should happen that they did beget and rear children, these in their turn would show even less love for their parents, because they would not see the love that they had for them in their hearts, since it is invisible. Such a state of affairs would result if those things which cannot be seen are not the object of a praiseworthy faith but instead are recklessly and rashly believed.

What am I to say about those other ties existing between brothers, sisters, sons-in-law, fathers-in-law, and any other kind of blood relationship and of bonds between friends, if the love and goodwill of children for parents and of parents for their children remains unsure and dubious? And is a kindness which is obligatory to go unreciprocated or not to be considered obligatory, since what cannot be seen in another person is not believed to exist? Furthermore, caution of this kind is not clever but despicable, when we refuse to believe we are loved because we cannot see

---

4. In these two sentences Augustine uses three words for the one word translated here as "love"— *caritas, dilectio* and *amor*.

this love for ourselves, and we do not return it to those to whom we believe it is not due. The consequence of our refusal to believe what we cannot see is that human relationships are thrown into chaos, and foundations are utterly swept away by our failure to trust the goodwill of people, a goodwill which is impossible for us to actually see.

I refrain from mentioning how numerous is that particular class of people who find fault with us for believing things we cannot see, yet who themselves give credence to tradition and history and even to places they have never visited. Such people do not assert, "We withhold belief because we have not seen it for ourselves." Were they to make such a statement, they would be compelled to admit that the identity of their parents was a matter of doubt, for they have believed this on the basis of what others have told them, who were not in a position to demonstrate a fact which already belonged to the past. Of themselves they retain no awareness of the period in question; nonetheless they are prepared to give their assent unhesitatingly to others who told them about it. For unless this were the case, and as long as we evade a bold act of faith in those things we cannot see, an upsurge of faithless impiety against parents would be the inevitable outcome.[5]

3, 4. If therefore human society itself could not endure because of our refusal to believe what we could not see, and in view of the disappearance of mutual harmony, how much more credence ought to be given to those divine matters which remain unseen! And, if this credence were not forthcoming, not only would certain human friendships suffer profanation but so would even the most supreme form of religion itself, with the direst possible consequences.[6]

5. "But," you will retort, "although I may be unable to see the goodwill of my friend, I can still discover this through numerous proofs; whereas, for your part, you, who would have us believe things we cannot see, fail to give us any proofs." However, it is no small concession for you to admit that there are certain things which, although not visible, must still be believed because of

---

5. See *Confessions* VI, 5, 7.
6. This argument presupposes an initial faith in eternal life.

certain clear proofs. Consequently, we are agreed on the fact that we are not to refrain from believing everything we cannot see, and that opinion, which maintains that we are in no way bound to believe what we cannot see, lies discredited and disproved.

Yet those people who allege that our faith in Christ lacks any proof are greatly mistaken. For what proofs could be clearer than the ones which were foretold and which we now see come true? You, then, who think that no visible proofs exist which would enable you to believe in Christ, should pay attention to the things you can actually see.

The Church herself addresses you with words of maternal love: "I, whose ongoing fruitfulness and growth throughout the whole world you admire, once did not exist as you see me now, but *in your offspring all the nations shall be blessed* (Gn 22:18). By conferring a blessing on Abraham, God was at the same time promising me; in consequence of the blessing given to Christ, I am spread through all the nations. The sequence of generations testifies that Christ is the seed of Abraham. Let me recall briefly that Abraham was the father of Isaac, Isaac the father of Jacob, and Jacob the father of the twelve sons from whom arose the people of Israel. Jacob himself was also called Israel. One of his twelve sons was Judah, whence the name of the Jewish people, from whom was born the Virgin Mary, who bore Christ. And look: you see and are amazed at the fact that all nations are blessed in Christ, that is, in the seed of Abraham, and still you are afraid to believe in Christ, someone you ought to fear rather than believe in!

"Or could it be that you doubt or balk at the virgin birth, a truth that you ought to believe was appropriate to the birth of the God-man? Believe also what was foretold by the prophet: *Behold, a virgin shall conceive in her womb and bear a son, and he shall be called Emmanuel, which means God-with-us* (Is 7:14). Therefore, have no doubts about the virgin giving birth, if you wish to have faith in the birth of God who, without abdicating his governance of the world, came in the flesh to humankind, bestowing fecundity on his mother, yet not taking away her integrity.

"If he was always God, it was entirely fitting that he should be born a man in this way and by such a birth become God for us. To this God the prophet speaks again: *Your throne, O God, shall last from age to age; a scepter of justice is the scepter of your kingdom. You have loved justice and hated evil; therefore, God, your God, has anointed you with the oil of gladness above your peers.* (Ps 44:7-8)[7] The anointing spoken of here, where God anointed God, is a spiritual one, referring to the Father's anointing of the Son. Consequently, we acknowledge that Christ is derived from chrism, which means anointing.

"I am the Church, about whom it is spoken to him in the same psalm and foretold as a deed to be accomplished: *The queen stands on your right hand, adorned in garments of gold and varied clothing* (Ps 44:10), that is, in the mystery of wisdom, clothed with a diversity of languages. There it is said to me: *Listen, daughter, and pay heed and give ear, forget your own people and your father's house, because the king has desired your beauty; for he is the Lord your God, and the daughters of Tyre shall worship him with gifts, all the richest of the land shall seek your presence. All the glory of the king's daughter is within; she is arrayed in cloth-of-gold. Virgins shall be led to the king after her, those who are her companions shall be brought to you; they shall be led amid joy and gladness, and brought into the king's temple. Sons have been born to you in place of your fathers; you shall establish them as princes throughout the whole earth. They shall make your name remembered from one generation to the next; therefore the nations shall praise you for ever and ever.* (Ps 44:11-18)

6. "If you yourselves are unable to recognize even now this queen, fertile with royal offspring; if she fails to see fulfilled the promise made to her, *Listen, daughter, and pay heed;* if she, to whom it was said, *Forget your own people and your father's house,* has not willingly rejected those observances of this world which previously obtained; if she, to whom it was said, *The king has desired your beauty, for he is the Lord your God,* does not confess Christ as Lord in every part of the world; if she does not witness the nations of the world offering prayers to Christ

---

7. See also the detailed christological and ecclesiological interpretation of Ps 44 in *The City of God* XVII, 16, and in *Exposition of Psalm 44.*

and bringing him gifts, the one of whom it was said to her, *The daughters of Tyre shall worship him with gifts;* if it is not evident that the rich lay aside their pride and beg help from the Church, she whom the psalm addresses, *All the richest of the land shall seek your presence;* if the daughter of the queen, who has been commanded to pray, *Our Father, who art in heaven* (Mt 6:9), goes unrecognized and says this of her holy ones, *Our inner man is being renewed day by day* (2 Cor 4:16); if all the glory of the queen's daughter is within after his good odor is spread in every place[8] and consecrated virgins are not brought to Christ, and it is not she who is addressed and referred to as follows, *Virgins shall be led to the king after her, those who are her companions shall be brought to you;* and lest 'being led' might suggest captivity in some prison, the text continues, *They shall be led amid joy and gladness, and brought into the king's temple;* if she fails to bring forth sons, who shall be appointed rulers by her everywhere, like fathers, she to whom it has been said, *Sons shall be yours in place of your fathers; you shall establish them as princes throughout the whole earth,* and who, being a mother and both superior and subject, commends herself to their prayers, which explains what follows, *They shall make your name remembered from one generation to the next;* if, because of the preaching of these same fathers who make his name forever remembered, such great numbers of people do not gather and give praise ceaselessly to his grace, he to whom it is said, *Therefore the nations shall praise you for ever and ever—*

4, 6. "If these things are not clear beyond doubt, so that our opponents do not know where to look to avoid being overcome by the same force of argument and consequently find themselves forced to admit that they are obvious, you would in that case perhaps have good reason to retort that you see no proofs which would compel you to believe in what you cannot see. But were it to happen that the things you now can see, which have been long foretold and are now most clearly coming to pass; if truth itself resounds both through the word of ancient prophets and then

8. See 2 Cor 2:15.

with subsequent dramatic fulfillment—O vestiges of unbelief! blush at what you can clearly see, so that you may believe in those things you cannot see.[9]

7. "Pay heed to me," the Church is saying to you, "pay heed to me whom you can see, even if you do not want to see. Those faithful people who were present in Judea at that particular time learned directly of the virgin-birth, the miracles, the passion, resurrection and ascension of Christ, and of all those divine utterances and deeds of his. You did not witness these events and so refuse to believe them. Therefore consider these facts, weigh them up carefully, ponder on what you can see, for they are not narrated to you as past events, nor predicted as things yet to come, but are proved to be a present reality.

"Or does it appear absurd and inconsequential to you, and the divine testimony of little or no worth at all in your estimation, that the whole human race flocks to the name of a single crucified man?[10] You did not see what was foretold and brought to pass regarding the human birth of Christ, *Behold, a virgin shall conceive in her womb and bear a son*, yet you do see how the promise made to Abraham has been fulfilled, *In your offspring all the nations of the earth shall be blessed.*

"You did not see what was foretold about the miracles of Christ and what has come to pass, *Come and consider the works of the Lord, the wonderful deeds he has done on the earth* (Ps 45:9), but you do see what was foretold, *The Lord said to me, You are my Son, today I have begotten you; ask me, and I will give you the nations for your inheritance, and the ends of the earth for your possession* (Ps 2:7-8).

"You did not see what was foretold and fulfilled about the passion of Christ,[11] *They have pierced my hands and my feet, and have numbered all my bones; they stared at me and fixed their gaze upon me; they divided my clothing among them and cast lots for my robe* (Ps 21:17-19), yet you do see what that same psalm foretold and what now clearly has reached fulfillment, *All*

9. See *Answer to Faustus, a Manichean* XIII, 1, 14.
10. See section 7,10; *The City of God* XXII, 5.
11. See *The City of God* XVII, 17.

*the ends of the earth shall remember and return to the Lord, and
all the nations of the world shall pay homage in his presence;
for the kingdom belongs to the Lord and he shall rule over the
nations* (Ps 21:28-29).

"You did not see what was foretold about the resurrection
of Christ and is now fulfilled, *They went outside and began to
speak; all my enemies whispered together about me and thought
evil against me; they engaged in evil talk against me* (Ps 40:7-9).
Showing that they achieved nothing by killing him who would
rise again, the psalmist goes on to say, *Will the one who sleeps
not succeed in rising again?* (Ps 40:9) And further on in the same
prophecy, having foretold the role of the traitor, which is also recorded in the gospel, as follows, *The one who ate at my table has
raised his heel against me,* the psalmist immediately adds, *But
you, Lord, have mercy on me and I will repay them* (Ps 40:11).
This is precisely what has been fulfilled: Christ fell asleep but
reawakened; in other words, he died and rose again. Speaking in
the same prophetic way he says in another psalm, *I fell asleep and
took my rest, but I arose because the Lord upheld me* (Ps 3:6).

"I concede that you may not have seen any of this, but you
see his Church, about which the following prediction was both
made and fulfilled: *To you, Lord my God, shall the nations come
from the ends of the earth and declare, Our fathers did indeed
worship false idols, and in them there was no profit* (Jer 16:19).
Willing or unwilling, this you can certainly see, and if you still
labor under the impression that there ever was profit in these idols,
or still could be, then you can surely hear the exclamation of those
countless nations of the world, which have abandoned, discarded
or destroyed vanities of this kind, *Our fathers did indeed worship
false idols, and in them there was no profit; if human beings devise
their own gods, in truth they are not gods at all* (Jer 16:19-20).

"Because the text states, *To you shall the nations come from the
ends of the earth,* you must not think this prophecy implies that
the nations are to gather at the abode of some god. Grasp, as far as
you can, that when the peoples of the world come to the God of the
Christians, the supreme and true God, they do so not by walking
but by believing. Indeed, this very fact was foretold by another
prophet when he said, *The Lord shall prevail against them and*

destroy all the gods of the nations; and each from his own place, the islands of the nations, shall worship him (Zep 2:11). Jeremiah had expressed it this way, *To you shall the nations come,* while Zephaniah declared, *Each from his own place shall worship him.* They shall therefore come to him without leaving their own place, because by believing in him they will find him in their own heart.

"You have not seen what was foretold about Christ's ascension and then brought to fulfillment, *O God, be exalted above the heavens,* but you see what immediately follows, *And let your glory shine over the whole earth* (Ps 107:6).

"You have not seen all these prophecies which referred to Christ and have now been accomplished and completed, but you do not deny the present reality within his Church of all these other things. We have pointed out to you how both sets of events have been foretold, yet we are unable to show you visibly both sets of prophecies now fulfilled—because to recall the past for inspection is beyond our power."

5, 8. Yet, just as the good dispositions of our friends, though unseen, are considered trustworthy because of visible proofs, so in similar fashion the present visible reality of the Church is demonstrated in those writings where she is also foretold. Moreover, she is the proof of past prophecies and the herald of things yet to come, both of which are unseen. The reason for this is that past prophecies, which can no longer be seen, and those of the future, which still remain to be seen, as well as those of the present, which can now be seen—all of these lay in the future when they were first foretold, and not a single one of them at that time could be seen. When, therefore, these predictions began to be fulfilled, beginning from those which have already come to pass up to those which, foretelling Christ and his Church, are at present being fulfilled—they unfolded in orderly sequence. Included in this same sequence are prophecies about the day of judgment, the resurrection of the dead, the eternal damnation of the wicked with the devil, and the eternal happiness of the just with Christ, which were similarly predicted and will come to pass.

Why is it, then, that we refuse to believe the first and the last things, which we do not see, although we have as witnesses of both the things midway between them, which we do see? I am referring to those prophetic writings in which we either hear or read how these first, middle and last things were foretold before they come to pass. Unless perhaps people of no faith are under the impression that matters of this kind were put into writing by Christians, in order that those other things, which they do not believe or fail to see, might possess greater authority if the belief existed that they had already been promised before they came to pass.

6. 9. If they suspect this to be the case, they should turn their attention to the writings of our Jewish opponents.[12] There they can read for themselves either those facts which we have recalled or numerous other ones which we have not mentioned and are almost too many to be counted. These prophecies have been foretold of Christ, the one in whom we believe, and of the Church to which we cling, from the time of faith's laborious beginnings right up until the eternal happiness of the kingdom. But when they do peruse the texts in question they show no amazement that those Jews who possess the writings fail to understand them, because their powers of understanding are darkened through hostility. For those same prophets had warned beforehand that the Jewish people would not understand, that the other prophecies had to be fulfilled in a hidden way, and that in the just judgment of God a fitting punishment would be imposed on this same people. Yet the one whom they crucified and gave gall and vinegar to drink, although hanging on the cross for their sake so as to lead them from darkness into light, exclaimed, *Father forgive them, for they do not know what they are doing* (Lk 23:34). However, because of those others, whom for more hidden reasons he would abandon, he had foretold long before, through the prophet, *For food they offered me gall and gave me vinegar to drink. May their table become a trap for them, an occasion of vengeance and a stumbling-block. May their eyes grow dim so that they are unable to see, may their back be always bent.* (Ps 68:22-24) Despite such compelling proofs in support of what we believe, they go around with impaired vision so that, while one group of people brings the prophecies to fulfillment, this results in the other group's being condemned.

---

12. See *Exposition of Psalm* 56, 9: "A Jew carries the book which is the foundation of faith for a Christian" (trans. Boulding); *The City of God* XVIII, 46; *Answer to Faustus, a Manichean* XIII, 11.

Therefore it has come about instead that they would not be destroyed, lest this same sect be completely obliterated, but that, having been scattered throughout the world, they would bring these prophecies which tell of God's grace to us. The outcome of this is both a more robust refutation of unbelievers and a widespread source of good to us. You must take to heart this very point I am making, as has been prophesied, *Do not slay them, lest they forget your law; disperse them by your power* (Ps 58:12). The reason why they are not slain, therefore, does not lie in their forgetfulness of what they have read and heard. For, were they to forget completely the sacred scriptures, although they might not understand them, they would be slain by reason of that Jewish ritual itself because, being totally ignorant of the law and prophets, their Jewishness would be of no advantage to them. Consequently they have not been slain but dispersed, and, although they do not possess the faith which could save them, yet the memories they cling to are a source of help to us.[13] In their discourse they oppose us, with their books they support us. In their hearts they are hostile to us, yet they bear witness by their writings.

7, 10. Even were we to suppose that no prior prophetic witnesses existed pertaining to Christ and the Church, what person would not be immediately impelled to believe that the divine splendor had indeed burst forth upon humanity when he sees how false gods are now abandoned and their images smashed, their temples destroyed or put to another use,[14] and the empty rituals for so long part of human habit discontinued, while the one true God is invoked by the whole human race? And all this took place through one man who was mocked, arrested, bound, scourged, beaten, insulted, crucified, scorned and put to death!

Those disciples he chose to proclaim his teaching were simple and uneducated persons and fishermen and tax-collectors. They proclaimed his resurrection and ascension into heaven, which

---

13. See *Exposition of Psalm* 58, serm. 1, 22; *Answer to Faustus, a Manichean* XIII, 10.
14. The law distinguished between idols and temples. The former had to be destroyed, but buildings for worship could be retained and used for other purposes. See the *Theodosian Code* 16, 19, 18 (399); 16, 10, 19 (408). In Hippo, for example, the temple of the Phoenician Dea Celestis was transformed into the Christian Basilica Honoriana. See Sermon 162, 1-2; Letter 232, 2.

they declared they had seen for themselves, and, filled with the Holy Spirit, they gave voice to this gospel in all manner of languages which they had never learned. The crowd that heard them partly believed, while the remainder, refusing to believe, resisted stubbornly. These disciples thus fought to death for the truth, declining to repay evil with evil, and were victorious by dying rather than by killing.

As you see, the world has been transformed by this religion. To this gospel human hearts have likewise turned: the hearts of men and women, of people great and small, of learned and ignorant, of wise and foolish, of powerful and weak, those of noble and those of common birth, those of exalted and those of lowly estate. Spread throughout the world, such has been the manner of the Church's growth that no sect or any kind of anti-Christian error arises which does not have glorying in the name of Christ as its aim and aspiration.[15] Indeed, unless adverse movements of this sort exercised a healthy restraint they would not be permitted to spring up in the world.[16]

How could that crucified one possibly have accomplished so much, if not for the fact that God had assumed human nature, even supposing he had not foretold any of these future events through the prophets? But since so wonderful a mystery of love had its own earlier prophets and heralds who prophesied in God's name that he was to come,[17] and he did come as foretold, who then could be so deranged as to assert that the apostles lied about Christ? For they proclaimed that he had indeed come, just as the prophets had earlier foretold that he would. Nor did the prophets remain silent about the future as far as the apostles were concerned, for they had this to say about the apostles: *No speech, no word of theirs goes unheard; their sound has gone forth through all the earth and their words to the ends of the world* (Ps 18:4-5). Without a doubt we see this prophecy fulfilled in the world, even if we did not see Christ in the flesh. What person, therefore, unless mentally blinded through some astonishing ailment, or

15. See Letter 118, 12; *Faith and the Creed* 21.
16. See 1 Cor 11:19; *True Religion* 6, 10.
17. See 1 Tm 3:16.

very coarse and unfeeling, could refuse to believe in those sacred writings which predicted that the whole world would one day believe?

8, 11. As for you, my dear people, let this faith be nurtured and increase within you, a faith which you already have, or have only lately, embraced. For just as those temporal events long since foretold have come to pass, so likewise will those promises of eternity come to fulfillment. Do not allow yourselves to be misled either by arrogant pagans or deceitful Jews or erroneous heretics or even ill-disposed Christians within the Church itself, who as enemies are all the more harmful because they come from within. The divine prophecies in this regard are not silent, for fear that those who are weak in faith should be unduly disturbed, for in the Song of Songs Christ the bridegroom addresses his bride the Church in these words, *As a lily among the thorns, so is my beloved among daughters* (Sg 2:2). He does not say "among strangers" but *among daughters.*

He who has ears to hear should hear (Mt 13:9); and, while the net which was cast into the sea collects fish of every kind, as the holy gospel relates, and is being hauled to the shore, in other words to the end of the world, people should separate themselves from the bad fish in their hearts, not in their body. This they do by changing their wicked ways and not tearing asunder the holy nets.[18] If it appears that those who have been tried and tested intermingle at present with the wicked, the reason is that, when the separation takes place on the shore, it is not punishment they will receive but everlasting life.[19]

---

18. The implicit exhortation to remain within the unity of the Church may be a sign of the continuing effects of the Donatist controversy.
19. See Mt 13:47-49.

The Advantage of Believing

Translation by Ray Kearney
Introduction and notes
by Michael Fiedrowicz

Introduction

1. Occasion and Addressee of the Work

"When I was now a presbyter at Hippo Regius I wrote a book on the advantage of believing to a friend of mine who had been deceived by the Manicheans. I knew that he was still being held captive by that error and was making fun of the teaching of the Catholic faith, because people were commanded to believe but were not taught that was true by the surest reasoning."[1] Augustine's first publication after priestly ordination was written between the beginning of 391 and August 392.[2] An event of his own past still preoccupied him: together with his friends Alypius, Romanianus, and Honoratus, he had endorsed Manicheanism. Since then, Alypius had followed him and converted to the Catholic faith. Meanwhile, Romanianus had in his hands the work entitled *True Religion*. Only Honoratus remained tied to Manicheanism.[3]

Initially, indeed, Honoratus had rejected that teaching but at Augustine's urging had looked into it more closely and had then joined the Manicheans. As is clear from the personal reminiscence in *The Advantage of Believing* 1, 2, the attraction of Manicheanism for the two student friends was its claim to give a scientific, rational explanation of all reality. Although Honoratus was not a Christian by birth, he made his own the rejection of the Catholic Church on the

---

1. *Revisions* I, 14, 1.
2. On the work see A. Hoffmann, *Augustins Schrift "De utilitate credendi." Eine Analyse* (Münster 1997); O. Grassi, "Per una scoperta del *De utilitate credendi*," in *"De vera religione," "De utilitate credendi," "De fide rerum quae non videntur"* (Rome 1994) 11-30.
3. On Honoratus see F. Decret, *L'Afrique Manichéenne I* (Paris: Études Augustiniennes, 1978) 72-77, 378-379.

grounds that its call for faith and its subordination to authority did not meet the Manichean ideal. In addition, the Church held fast to the Old Testament, which in the Manichean view could not stand up to critical questioning. Honoratus was soon a convinced Manichean.

When Augustine went off to Rome the friends lost contact, but after his return to North Africa he felt obliged to repair, as best he could, the harm which he had formerly caused the soul of this friend of his youth. *The Advantage of Believing* is thus a work written in a very personal tone. "You, who are my special concern,"[4] is the way Augustine addresses the friend of his youth, and it is the intellectual abilities, rhetorical training, and critical mind of this friend that determine the line of argument, the themes, and the structure of the work. In places the account turns into an implicit dialogue that is meant to overcome the reservations and resistances of a mentality that had once ruled Augustine himself.

But the work is not simply a purely personal conversation among friends. Augustine is also writing for a wider circle of readers. In the person of Honoratus the North African Manicheans are also being addressed, as are all who had come in contact with their propaganda against the Catholic Church.

2. Purpose of the Work

The Advantage of Believing has a strictly limited goal. In his final chapter Augustine says expressly that he intended neither a refutation of Manicheanism nor a comprehensive presentation of Catholic teaching. "I only wanted to weed out from you, if I could, the false opinions about Christian truths that were instilled in us through malice or ignorance and to raise your mind to learn certain great truths about God."[5] Augustine's concern was thus primarily protreptic or exhortatory. He wanted to "turn" his friend to the Catholic faith. But in order to win him over to that faith, he had first to overcome the negative prejudice of a Manichean against the views of the Church.

Honoratus was especially critical of the Catholic Church's demand for faith and its retention of the Old Testament. On the

4. *The Advantage of Believing* 1, 3.
5. Ibid. 18, 36.

one hand, then, the issue was the method of appropriating truth; on the other, it was the valid method of interpreting texts. Before there could be any discussion of doctrinal content, fundamental questions of methodology had to be clarified. This requirement gave the work a further apologetical, anti-Manichean intention.

Augustine wanted to win Honoratus over to the Catholic Church by showing that the Church's position on both of these questions of method was the correct one. At the same time, these explanations would protect other Christians against Manichean propaganda. The entire set of arguments thus aims at a defense of the Catholic Church against Manichean attacks. Manicheanism as the opposing position is always in mind.

In addition, Augustine was pursuing a personal apologetical goal. About five years earlier, when still a supporter of the Manicheans, he himself had successfully defended their views in public debates with Catholic Christians.[6] He desired, therefore, to explain to his fellow believers the reasons for his change from Manicheanism to the Church. He also had to forestall an a priori condemnation of himself by Manicheans such as Honoratus, if he were to get any hearing at all from them. For the Manicheans rejected anyone who had turned away from them: their judgment was that "the light has passed through that person."[7] Augustine had therefore to make plausible his personal reasons for thus turning away. It is to this concern that we owe one of the first descriptions of the path Augustine followed in his conversion.[8]

Even here, however, there was no question solely of a personal justification of Augustine against Manichean criticism. Rather, using himself as an example, he sketches in *The Advantage of Believing* 8, 20 the process which he wishes to initiate in Honoratus by means of his book. In describing the path he himself followed, he is describing the path which the friend of his youth also followed to some extent. When he harks back to his journey through the Manichean error that led him away from the religion of his childhood.[9] he is beginning

---

6. See *The Two Souls* 11.
7. *The Advantage of Believing* 1, 3.
8. See P. Courcelle, *Recherches sur les Confessions de saint Augustin* (Paris 1968) 269-290.
9. *The Advantage of Believing* 7, 17.

to describe his subsequent return to the Christian religion[10] and to justify it. His friend has plenty of opportunity to raise his objections; Augustine intends, step by step, to move his friend forward by argument and lead him to the same goal.[11]

3. Structure of the Work

Criteria both of content and of language and form reveal the following structure:

Introduction (1, 1-2, 4)

Part I. The problem being discussed (3, 5-6, 13)
> First line of argument: Possible methods of interpreting the Bible (3, 5-9)
> Second line of argument: Sources of possible error in interpreting the text (4, 10-5, 12)
> Conclusion: Arguments against Augustine's rejection of the Old Testament while he was a Manichean (6, 13)

Part II. The problem of belief (7, 14-17, 35)
> The search for truth in human life (7, 14-8, 20)
> Belief as an indispensable way of acquiring truth (9, 21 14, 32)
> The necessary acceptance of an authority (15, 33-17, 35)
Conclusion (18, 36)

4. The Interpretation of Scripture

The Manicheans accused the Catholic Church of dealing uncritically with the Bible. The accounts of creation (they said) were contradictory; the existence of evil (*malum*) could not be explained if only a single, good creator God were accepted; God did not in fact have anthropomorphic features or negative emotions; the so-called "just" of the Old Testament acted immorally; there was no connec-

---

10. Ibid. 8, 20.
11. See A. Hoffmann, " 'Ich will dir zeigen, welchen Weg ich genommen habe...' (Aug., *util cred* 20). Zur Funktionierung der eigenen Vita in Augustins Schrift *De utilitate credendi*," in B. Czapka, ed., *Vir bonus dicendi peritus. Festschrift A. Weische* (Wiesbaden 1997) 165-80.

tion between the Old Testament and the New, because the theological content and ethical directives of the two were compatible.

Augustine met these attacks with two arguments. First, he argued on the basis of the theory of the four methods of exegesis.[12] The Manichean critique of the Old Testament was improper because it presupposed that biblical statements had only a literal sense. Instead, Augustine says, there are four ways of interpreting scriptural passages. Historical exegesis aims at ascertaining the content of a text or story; etiological exegesis brings to light the basis of an event or saying; analogical exegesis establishes the agreement between the two Testaments; and allegorical exegesis looks for the figurative meaning of a text, whenever it becomes clear that the text is not to be understood literally. Augustine used this theory from the Greek tradition about two years later in *The Literal Meaning of Genesis*, but after that it is not used again in his writings. Consequently, Augustine's thoughts on the subject represent only a transitional phase. Only later on, in *Teaching Christianity*, will he develop his own self-contained theory of interpretation.

In a second argument he analyzed the various ways in which a text might be wrongly understood.[13] The purpose of this survey was to prove that none of the possible kinds of error applied to the Church's interpretation of the scriptures and that the Manichean criticism was unfounded.[14] Catholic Christians did not understand the texts of the Bible in the way which the Manicheans attributed to them, nor did the Old Testament writings have the meaning which the Manicheans assumed in their attacks. Instead, the Catholic interpretation of the Old Testament proves exemplary for the correct reading of a text that is given in *The Advantage of Believing* 5, 11; that is, a true text is rightly understood. Right understanding, however, presupposes a fundamental "sympathy" with the author.[15] Augustine and Honoratus had sinned against this hermeneutical principle in their youthful reading of the Old Testament by reading it with the negative outlook of the Manicheans or, in other words,

---

12. *The Advantage of Believing* 3, 5-9.
13. Ibid. 4, 10-5, 12.
14. See C. Schäublin, "Augustin, *De utilitate credendi*: Über das Verhältnis des Interpreten zum Text," *Vigiliae Christianae* 43 (1989) 53-68.
15. *The Advantage of Believing* 6, 13.

by choosing Manichean critics as interpreters of the Old Testament. In contrast, Augustine reminds his friend of the rule that holds for every kind of literature: to let an author's writings be explained by his disciple but not by his critic. A better and deeper understanding results from a connaturality with the text and its author.

5. The Problem of Belief

Honoratus' second prejudice against the Catholic Church was that it was hostile to reason. It is clear that in North Africa the Manicheans encountered Catholic Christians who had little schooling in the things of the mind and were unwilling or unable to defend their convictions with rational arguments. Instead, they demanded that doctrinal statements be believed, that is, accepted as true, without having any rational insight into them. The Manicheans, on the contrary, rejected belief as a rash acceptance of something as true on inadequate grounds; in fact, Faustus even attributed to his Catholic opponent scruples about using the natural gift of reason.[16] The Manicheans built upon rational insight and discussion, not on authorities and the obedience of faith. In their view, by reducing all events to the two principles of the Good and the Evil, the teaching of Mani offered a reasonable and even scientific explanation of all reality. According to *The Advantage of Believing* (14, 31), then, the Manichean position can be summed up in the statement: "It is wrong to believe anyone without proof."[17]

Augustine saw in these objections, too, a problem of methodology that had to be clarified before any discussion of content. Therefore the "belief" to which reference is made in the title of the work is not "belief" as the totality of contents and assertions, but rather "believing" as a personal act. The basic issue is the way in which the individual person achieves possession of truth. Against the Manicheans Augustine defended his conviction that rational knowledge alone cannot provide this access to truth. Instead, belief is the first, necessary step. For this reason he applies himself to giving a rational basis for belief as a method of appropriating truth.

First of all, he discusses the necessity of the quest for truth, as well as the best point of departure for the quest. The claim that

---

16. See *Answer to Faustus, a Manichean* XVIII, 3.
17. *The Advantage of Believing* 7, 14-8, 20.

the soul finds itself in a state of error and ignorance is one that even Honoratus, a Manichean, can accept. Then, since the soul's salvation and at the same time its greatest happiness require knowledge of truth, the soul must look for a way to truth. The quest for truth is simultaneously a quest for God and also for the true religion as the "veneration and knowledge of God." Now, at what point shall the soul begin this quest? As they seek, human beings are faced with a multiplicity of incompatible offers of truth. Which shall seekers choose? What are the norms to guide their choice? The problem is that they themselves do not yet know the truth and therefore cannot judge whether or not the truth claims of a thinker or an institution are justified.

In response to this difficulty Augustine sets down as a criterion the outward success of a doctrine, that is, its reputation, the number of its followers, and its spread. This principle rests on the premise that truth, or, in this case, the true religion, has an inner power to win through. It is with this criterion in view that Augustine recommends the Catholic Church as the starting point of the quest (in *The Advantage of Believing* 7, 19). The choice among religions (Christian, Jewish, cults of pagan divinities) must fall on the Christian, because Christians are in the majority. Among Christian groups (Catholics, heretics) the Catholic Church must be given priority because it is numerically the largest group and therefore can alone be called "all-embracing," whereas heretics have each their special names. In keeping with Augustine's premise, the Catholic Church offers the best promise of success in the search for truth.

In *The Advantage of Believing* 8, 20, Augustine concludes the points made thus far by describing the course he himself had followed, and he deals next with the decisive problem: the method for appropriating the truth. The proof that the knowledge gained by reason alone is insufficient for finding the truth and that belief is indispensable makes it clear that the method of the Catholic Church is the only correct one. In 9, 21 Augustine formulates his principal thesis: In order to come to knowledge of the truth, it is necessary first to believe (that is, to accept as true statements which reason cannot yet grasp), to purify oneself morally, and, in both areas, to subject oneself to authentic authority.

Augustine gives both positive and negative arguments for the necessary temporal priority of belief before insight.[18] The first argument[19] vouches for believing by showing it to be rationally responsible and even necessary. Augustine uses the example of friendship to show how believing is indispensable in everyday life. An argument by analogy shows that belief is also necessary in the religious sphere. Belief is indispensable especially for the broad masses of human beings if they are to come to the knowledge of God. Since the majority of human beings do not have the needed philosophical training and since the salvation of the soul is involved when it comes to the knowledge of God, those without intellectual training must be led to the divine mysteries step by step along the way of belief.

The second, negative argument[20] is directed at non-belief, that is, in this anti-Manichean context, against the limitation of knowledge exclusively to rational insight. Using the relationship between parents and children as an example, Augustine proves his thesis that human society is impossible without belief. No one can be certain from experience who his parents are. Renunciation of belief destroys the basic cohesion of human society. Augustine sums up his thoughts in the statement: "I do not know how it is possible at all for someone not to believe anything."[21] Once again, an argument by analogy shows non-belief to be impossible in the religious sphere as well. All religious seekers already believe that what is being sought (God or the true religion) exists and can be found. Finally, a rejection of belief is openly contradictory to the demands of Christ.

By means of this double argument Augustine proves his positive thesis: "It is not unreasonable to believe," and his negative thesis: "It is unreasonable not to believe." In a final step (15, 33-17, 35) he shows the necessity of following an authority. He had earlier shown (12, 27-13, 28) that an ignorant person striving to know the truth is unconditionally dependent on the help of a wise person. At the same time, however, being ignorant, he cannot recognize the truth even in other people. The result is a dilemma, for he is caught between the necessity of following someone who is wise and the

18. Ibid. 9, 22-14, 32.
19. Ibid. 10, 23-24.
20. Ibid. 12, 26-14, 32.
21. Ibid. 10, 25.

impossibility of finding such a person. Augustine is convinced that divine authority alone can lead a human being out of this dilemma. God helped the ignorant when his Wisdom became a human being in Christ and acted with authority.

In Augustine's understanding of it, authority meant the ability to impress men and women and bind them to itself. Later on, this authority was transferred to the Church as Christ's representative in history. Looking back at his own conversion, Augustine once admitted: "I would certainly not have believed the gospel if the *auctoritas* of the Catholic Church had not moved me to do so."[22] In his eyes, it was chiefly miracles and worldwide success that won for Christ and the Church the authority, that is, the power, to prevail and to motivate human beings to change their behavior. Miracles and the throng of followers are not proofs of the possession of truth but they do lend credibility. It is this credibility that causes even the ignorant to follow the instructions of Christ and his Church and turn "from love of this world to the true God."[23]

6. The Importance of the Work

It is questionable whether Augustine's arguments moved Honoratus to convert to the Catholic Church. *The Advantage of Believing* was conceived as a work that would lead the addressee to take only the first step away from his mistaken Manichean path and in the right direction. A more detailed refutation of his errors is lacking, as is a more comprehensive introduction to the truths of the Catholic faith. These indicators suggest that Augustine did not achieve the desired result and that Honoratus closed his ears to the appeal Augustine so passionately addressed to him.

Yet this work, as Augustine's attempt to get something going with a person of a different faith,[24] remains of interest in that it appeals to the universal foundations of thought and builds further argument on them. The author adapts his arguments to the addressee's present comprehension in order then to break down his prejudices, which block any approach to the faith of the Catholic

---

22. *Answer to the Letter of Mani* 5.
23. *The Advantage of Believing* 16, 34
24. The Manicheans understood themselves to be Christians, and indeed the true Christians in whom alone the teaching of Christ found its full embodiment.

Church. In the process, the work gives a great deal of information on North African Manicheanism in the fourth century.

To the extent that Augustine often uses his own career as part of the argument, the work is an informative source for his intellectual biography. The personal details serve as an important point of reference for the accounts in his other writings, especially the *Confessions*. Equally clear are the influences, considerations, and discoveries that distanced him from the Manicheans and led him finally to the Catholic Church.

Theologically significant is the treatment of questions of hermeneutical methodology, which is valid not only for biblical exegesis but for all forms of textual interpretation. But it is above all Augustine's thoughts on the problem of the acquisition of truth and on the concept of faith that became influential in the history of theology. Specifically, he worked out the alternatives of rational insight and belief that were to form the basis of medieval Scholastic thought and that have remained relevant down to our day in determining the relationship between believing (*credere*) and knowing (*scire*). The defense of faith in this work does not signify any rejection of reason. Augustine's concern is rather to show a broader way to wisdom and ultimately to God which all human beings can follow in their history.

Augustine's merit consists not least in having analyzed the act of belief and having thus brought to light this element in the theory of knowledge. The act of belief or faith, too, can be shown by reason to be a form of human knowledge. Belief is not an alternative to knowledge but is a way of knowing realities that are not the objects of immediate and evident perception (*perceptio*). Belief is an acceptance of a truth that cannot be reached in any other way. Differently than in his early dialogues and in *True Religion*, Augustine was not satisfied here to urge the way of belief.[25] Rather he sought to explain the nature of the act of belief by analyzing the cognitive value of this way in the larger context of human knowing in general and by carefully distinguishing believing (*credere*) from, on the one hand, knowing based on evidence (*scire*) and imagined knowing (*opinari*) and, on the other, from gullibility (*credulitas*).

---

25. See ibid. 9, 22; 11, 25.

Revisions I, 14

One Book Addressed to Honoratus

1. When I was now a presbyter at Hippo Regius I wrote a book on the advantage of believing to a friend of mine who had been deceived by the Manicheans. I knew that he was still being held captive by that error and was making fun of the teaching of the Catholic faith, because people were commanded to believe but were not taught what was true by the surest reasoning.

In this book I said, "Although it is wrong now for Christians to observe those precepts and commandments of the law, such as the Sabbath and circumcision and sacrifices and the like, there is still much symbolism in them. Any devout person, therefore, understands that there is nothing more harmful than to take everything there according to the literal meaning of the words but that there is nothing more beneficial than to have it unveiled by the Spirit. So it is that *the letter kills but the spirit gives life* (2 Cor 3:6)."[1] But I have explained those words of the apostle Paul in another way and—as far as I can tell, or, rather, as appears from the things themselves—much more suitably in the book that is entitled *The Spirit and the Letter*,[2] although this understanding is also not to be rejected.

2. Again, I said, "In relation to religion there are two kinds of persons who deserve to be praised. The first is those who have already found it, and they must be considered the happiest; the other is those who are dedicated to the proper search for it.[3] The

---

1. 3,9.
2. See *The Spirit and the Letter* 5,7.
3. See Mt 7:7-8 par.

first have already arrived, while the others are on the path by
which they will surely arrive."[4] If those who, in these words of
mine, have already found, who I said had already arrived, are
held to be the happiest in such a way as not to be so in this life
but are such in the one for which we hope and to which we are
journeying along faith's path, then this understanding is not erroneous. For they are to be considered as having found what was
being sought for, and who are already where we desire to arrive
by seeking and believing—that is, by staying on faith's path. But
if they are thought to be, or to have been, such in this life, it
does not seem to me to be true, not because in this life there
is absolutely nothing true to be found that is discerned by the
mind rather than believed by faith but because, whatever it is, it
is not enough to confer the utmost happiness. It is not as though
what the Apostle refers to when he says, *We see now through
a mirror in obscurity*, and *Now I know partly* (1 Cor 13:12), is
not discernable by the mind. Of course it is discernable, but it is
not enough to confer the greatest happiness. What makes for the
greatest happiness is what is spoken of: *But then face to face*, and
Then I shall know as I have been known (1 Cor 13:12). Those
who have found this must be said to be abiding in the possession
of happiness, which the path of faith to which we are adhering
leads us to, and where we desire to arrive by believing. But who
those happiest ones are, who are already in possession of what
this path leads to, is a great question. To be sure, there is no question that the holy angels are there. But whether at least those holy
human beings who are now dead should be said to abide in its
possession is worth investigating. For now they have in fact been
stripped of the corruptible body that weighs down the soul,[5] but
they themselves also await the redemption of their body,[6] and
their flesh reposes in hope[7] and does not yet shine with its coming
incorruptibility. But whether, because of this, given that it says
face to face, they will be less capable of contemplating the truth

4. 11,25.
5. See Wis 9:15.
6. See Rom 8:23.
7. See Ps 15:9.

with the eyes of their heart, is not something that we can discuss and examine here.

Again, what I said, "To understand things that are important and good, or even divine, is the happiest thing,"[8] we must refer to that same happiness. For in this life, however much something may be known, it still does not confer the most happiness, because what is as yet unknown is incomparably greater.

3. And I said, "It matters a great deal whether something is ascertained by the secure mental reasoning that we call understanding, or whether for good reasons it is entrusted to oral tradition and writing for the belief of future generations."[9] And shortly thereafter I said, "What we understand comes from reason, what we believe comes from authority."[10] This must not be understood in such a way that, when speaking casually, we would be afraid of saying that we know something because we believe suitable witnesses. To be sure, when we speak properly, we say that we only know what we understand with the mind's firm reasoning. But when we speak in a way that corresponds to common usage, which is how even divine scripture speaks, we should not hesitate to say that we know both what we perceive with the senses of our body and what we believe through faith by means of worthy witnesses, as long as we understand, however, what a distinction there is between the one and the other.

4. Again, what I said, "No one will question that everyone is either foolish or wise,"[11] can seem to contradict what one may read in the third book of *Free Choice*: "It is as though human nature accepts no intermediate condition apart from foolishness and wisdom."[12] But that was said in that passage when there was a question about the first man, whether a wise man could become either foolish or neither [wise nor foolish], because in no way were we able to call a person foolish who was created without vice, given that foolishness is a great vice, and it was not very clear how we could call a person wise who was capable of being

8. 11,25.
9. Ibid.
10. Ibid.
11. 12,27.
12. Free Choice III,24,71.

led astray. Hence I tried to express the matter briefly by saying, "It is as though human nature would accept no intermediate condition apart from foolishness and wisdom." Indeed, I observed that we cannot say that infants as well, who we profess have contracted original sin but who do not yet make use of free choice either well or badly, are either wise or foolish. But I said at this point that all human beings were either wise or foolish—meaning those who already use reason, whereby human beings are distinguished from beasts—just as we say that all human beings want to be happy. Do we fear that in these words, which are so plain and clear, infants (who are as yet incapable of wanting this) would also be understood?

5. In another passage, when I was mentioning the miracles that the Lord Jesus performed when he was here in the flesh, I added this and said, "Why, you say, do these things not happen now?" And I replied, "Because they would not have any effect unless they caused wonder, and, if they were common occurrences, they would not cause wonder."[13] I said this because there are not such great nor so many [miracles] nowadays, not because none happen nowadays.[14]

6. At the end of the book I said, "As, however, our present discussion has lasted much longer that I thought it would, let us conclude the book here. I should like you to note that in it I have not yet begun to refute the Manicheans and have not yet started on that trivia, nor have I expanded on anything of substance about the actual Catholic teaching. I only wanted to weed out from you, if I could, the false opinions about Christian truths that were instilled in us through malice or ignorance and to raise your mind to learn certain great truths about God. That is why this volume is as it is. Now that your mind has been made more receptive, I shall perhaps move along more rapidly regarding other matters."[15] I did not say this as though up until then I had written nothing against the Manicheans or had committed to writing nothing about Catholic teaching, since so many previ-

---

13. 16,34.
14. See *Revisions* I,13,7 and note 215.
15. 18,36.

ously published volumes attest that I was not silent about either topic. But in this book, which was written for that man, I had not yet begun to refute the Manicheans and had not yet attacked that trivia, nor had I expanded on anything of substance about the actual Catholic teaching, because I was hoping that, once I had begun in this way, I was going to write to him what I had not yet written here.

This book begins in this way: "If I thought, Honoratus, that ... was just the same."

On the Advantage of Believing

1, 1. If I thought, Honoratus, that believing heretics was just the same as being a heretic, I do not think I would need to say anything on this subject, either in speech or in writing. These two things, however, are not the same at all. As I see it, a heretic is someone who is either the author of false and novel views or upholds them for the sake of some temporal gain, especially fame and power, whereas the person who believes someone like that is seduced by a veneer of truth and devotion. For this reason I felt I should not keep from you my thoughts about finding and holding to the truth. This, as you know, has been my burning passion since early youth.[1] It is, however, a subject far removed from the thoughts of shallow-minded persons, who have gone to extremes with material considerations and fallen into thinking that nothing exists except what they perceive with those five well-known sources[2] of information of the body. Even when they try to detach themselves from their senses, they still want to keep the deceits and images[3] they have garnered from them and think they can best assess the inexpressible innermost recesses of truth by their fatal and deceptive standards.

There is nothing easier, dear friend, than to say that one has discovered the truth, and even to think it, but from what I write here I am sure you will appreciate how difficult it really is. I have prayed to God, and I pray now, that it will be helpful, or at least not harmful, for you and anyone else at all into whose hands it

---

1. I.e., since Augustine read Cicero's *Hortensius*.
2. *Nuntiis*, literally "messengers." The senses are affected by things in the external world and "announce" this to the mind. See G. O'Daly, *Augustine's Philosophy of Mind* (London 1987) 80-105.
3. What seems to the senses to be true being is in fact only a weak reflection of the true, intelligible world.

chances to fall. This is what I hope for, knowing within myself that, in putting pen to paper now, I do so in a spirit of duty and devotion and not in pursuit of passing fame or shallow display.

2. My object then is to prove to you, if I can, that, when the Manicheans attack those who, before they are capable of gazing on that truth which is perceived by a pure mind, accept the authority of the Catholic faith and by believing are strengthened and prepared for the God who will bestow light, they are acting irrationally and sacrilegiously.

You know, Honoratus, that the only reason we fell in with them is because they declared with awesome authority, quite removed from pure and simple reasoning, that if any persons chose to listen to them they would lead them to God and free them from all error. What was it that for almost nine years drove me to disdain the religion that had been instilled in me as a child by my parents[4] and to follow those people and listen attentively to them[5] except that they said that we were held in fear by superstition[6] and that faith was imposed on us before reason, whereas they did not put pressure on anyone to believe without first discussing and explaining the truth? Who would not be enticed by promises like that, especially if it was the mind of a young man yearning for the truth and made proud and outspoken by the debates in the classes of certain scholars? That is how they found me at that time, scornful of the "old wives' tales" and keen to have and to imbibe the open, uncontaminated truth that they promised. What considerations held me back, and kept me from fully committing myself to them, and made me stay at the stage they called "hearer,"[7] not yet putting aside the hopes and concerns of this world except

4. See *Answer to the Skeptics* II, 2, 5; *The Two Souls* 1; *Confessions* I, 11, 17.
5. I. e., from his nineteenth to his twenty-eighth year (373-382). See *Confessions* IV, 1, 1: "nine years." More accurately it was not nine years but more than ten, since in 384 Augustine was thirty when he came in contact with the Manicheans in Rome, but with hardly any conviction left in him.
6. In *The Happy Life* 1, 4 Augustine tells of the superstition that kept him as a young man from the search for truth. By "superstition" he understood the simple popular piety such as his mother, for example, practiced.
7. The Manichean community was divided into the "elect" (*electi*), who were the officials and lived a strict ascetical life, and the "hearers" or "listeners" (*auditores*), who supported the elect but practiced renunciation only in a limited degree. See *Answer to Fortunatus, a Manichean* 3.

that I noticed that they themselves were for the most part full and lengthy in their refutation of others rather than steadfast and assured in rational support of their own position? What can I say about myself, already a Christian and Catholic as I was at the time? That, parched and almost overcome by prolonged thirst, crying and groaning, I shook off those things and pushed them away, and that I have now returned avidly to that breast? That, in the state I was in, I would imbibe from it what I needed to restore me and bring me back to the hope of life and salvation?

So what need I say about myself? You on the other hand were not yet a Christian, and, even though you expressed contempt for them, at my insistence you were reluctantly persuaded to listen to them and examine what they had to say. What was it that attracted you, I wonder? Was it not, I beg you to remember, a certain grand assumption and promise of proofs? Because they went on at such length arguing passionately about the mistakes of the uneducated (and I learned too late that for anyone with an average education this is so easy to do), if they introduced anything of their own errors, for want of any acceptable alternative we concluded that that was what we had to hold. In this way they did to us what cunning trappers are accustomed to do, when they fix branches smeared with birdlime alongside the water to deceive the thirsty birds. They bury and in various ways cover up the other branches around the water, or even scare the birds away from them with contraptions to frighten them, and so the birds fall into their traps not through choice but by default.

3. Why do I not give myself my own answer—that these eloquent, witty analogies and criticisms like these can be poured out with elegant sarcasm by any opponent against anyone who teaches anything? I thought, however, that I should include something like this in my writing as a warning to them to abandon their use of these methods. Then, just as he said, putting aside the common trivia, fact may compete with fact, case with case, proof with proof.[8] So let them stop saying the thing that seems to force itself to their lips when anyone who has listened to them for a long

---

8. See Cicero, *Academica* II, 25, 80; idem, *Pro Caelio* 9, 22.

time leaves them: "The light has passed through that person."[9] I am not too much worried about them, but you, who are my special concern, can see yourself how inane this is and how easy for anyone to answer. I leave its consideration, therefore, to your good sense. I have no fear that you will think that the light dwelled in me when I was caught up in the affairs of this world and pursued the ambitions of darkness, a beautiful wife, ostentatious wealth, empty honors and all the other dangerous and harmful pleasures. It is no secret to you that, when I was listening attentively to them, I did not cease to desire and hope for all this. It is not that I attribute this to their indoctrination; I even admit that they continually warned us to be on our guard against this. To say, however, that now, when I have turned away from all those shadows of reality[10] and have resolved to be content merely with the food and drink necessary for bodily health, the light has deserted me, whereas then, when I loved those shadows and was held ensnared by them, I was enlightened and shone with light—that, to put it as kindly as possible, is the statement of someone thinking too dimly about the subject but keen to talk about it. With your consent, however, let us move on to the topic.

2, 4. You are well aware that the Manicheans upset the uneducated by attacking the Catholic faith and especially by criticizing and tearing apart the Old Testament. They clearly do not appreciate how necessary it is to accept these and how beneficial it is for souls that are still crying babies, as it were, to drink from them and absorb them into the marrow of their bones.[11] There are certain things there that can be attacked in a popular way, on the grounds that they give offense to minds that are uninformed and unwary (which is the general majority). There are not many, however, who are able to defend them in a popular way through the symbolism they contain. The few who do have the knowledge to do this have no love for the publicity and particular competi-

---

9. *Kephalaia* 99, 9-17 (H. J. Polotsky and A. Böhlig, eds., *Manichäische Handschriften der Staatlichen Museen Berlin* 1 [Stuttgart 1940]).

10. Another allusion to the nature of the world perceptible to the senses as being only a reflection of reality. In the background is Plato's allegory of the cave; see his *Republic* 514a-518b.

11. See 1 Cor 3:2.

tion for honor of debates, and for that reason they are not known at all except to those who deliberately go looking for them.

With regard to this blunder of the Manicheans, in criticizing the Old Testament and the Catholic faith, I beg you to listen to my response to it. It is my hope and wish that you will take what I say in the spirit in which I say it. God, who knows the secrets of my conscience, knows there is no malice in what I write now, but I believe it has to be accepted in order to establish the truth. I have long since resolved to live only for this. I do so with extreme concern that I may very easily lead you astray with me, but at best it is very difficult to stay on the right path with you. I am confident, however, that he to whom I am consecrated[12] will not desert me even in this hope, that you will arrive with me on the path of wisdom. Day and night I strive to look upon him, and with the eye of my soul ravaged by the wounds of old opinions[13] I realize, often in tears, that because of my sins and ingrained habits I do not have the power. It is like what happens after a long period of blindness and darkness. Our eyes are barely open and they still reject the light, blinking at it and turning away from it, even though it is what they want—and most of all if anyone tries to show them the sun itself. It is like this now with me. I do not deny that there is something words cannot describe, the soul's one and only good, which is visible to the mind, and sighing and lamenting I confess I am not yet fit to gaze on it. He will not desert me because of this, provided I make nothing up, I am led by duty, I have love for the truth, I value friendship, I have great fear of your being deceived.

3, 5. The whole of the scripture that we call the Old Testament is offered to those who seriously wish to understand it under four aspects: as history, as explanation, as analogy, and as allegory. You must not think it is inappropriate for me to use Greek words.[14] In the first place, that is how I received it, and I would not presume to

---

12. The term "consecrated" (*sacratus*) is not a conclusive indication of Augustine's ordination as a priest of Hippo. As section 18 shows, the term applies also to Christians in general.

13. For "opinion" in the sense of "imagined knowledge" see section 25.

14. The Latin text here uses the Greek-derived words *historia, aetiologia, analogia* and *allegoria*. Among the precepts of rhetoric was the demand for *latinitas*, that is, in particular, the use of exclusively Latin words, but Quintilian, *Institutio oratorica* I, 5, 58, had already allowed the use of Greek words, when the required words were lacking in Latin.

convey it to you differently from the way I received it. Secondly, you will notice yourself that we have no commonly used names for these things, and it would surely be even less appropriate for me to make up names and define them. If, on the other hand, I employed circumlocutions, my discussion would be too cumbersome. I only ask you to believe that, whatever my mistakes, I do nothing from pride or arrogance.

Accordingly, there is the aspect of history, when we are taught what was written or what happened, or what did not happen but was written only as a story. There is the aspect of explanation, when we are shown the reasons why something was said or done. There is the aspect of analogy, when we are shown how the two testaments, the Old and the New, do not contradict each other. There is the aspect of allegory, when we are taught that what was written is not to be taken literally but has to be understood in a figurative sense.

6. Our Lord Jesus Christ and the apostles used all these methods. It was quoted from as history when the criticism was made that the disciples picked the ears of wheat on the Sabbath. *Have you not read what David did,* he said, *when he and his companions were hungry, how he went into the house of God and ate the loaves that were offerings, which it was not lawful for him and his companions to eat, but only the priests?* (Mt 12:3-4)

It relates to explanation when Christ said that a wife was not to be divorced except for the case of adultery and was told by those interrogating him that Moses allowed this, provided a document of dismissal was given. *Moses did this,* he said, *because of the hardness of your hearts* (Mt 19:8). Here the explanation is given of why it was right for Moses to allow that for the time being, so that the command which Christ gave could be seen as evidence that the times were now different. A detailed consideration of the differences between these two periods and the relation between them, designed and established in a wonderful plan of divine providence, would be very lengthy.

7. As for analogy, which enables the harmony between the two testaments to be perceived, what shall I say? It has been used by everyone whose authority those people recognize.[15] They

---

15. Jesus and the apostles are meant.

can ponder for themselves how much they usually say has been inserted in the sacred scriptures by some or other perverters of the truth.[16] Even when I listened to them, this assertion always seemed very weak indeed, and not only to me but to you too, as I well remember, and to all of us who were striving to form our opinions somewhat more carefully than the general crowd of believers. Much was expounded and explained to me, and I was very impressed by it. They were questions on which most of them showed off their skills, and the greater their assurance in the absence of any opposition the more effusive was their oratory. As I look back now, nothing they said seems so shameless or, to put it more gently, so uncritical and foolish as that the sacred scripture has been corrupted. They can offer no proof of this from any examples in recent memory. If they said they did not think they should accept those scriptures unreservedly because they were written by authors they do not believe wrote the truth, their rejection would at least be more direct and their error more human.

This is how they dealt with the book we call The Acts of the Apostles. When I reflect on this opinion of theirs, I cannot cease to be amazed. I am not looking for human wisdom here but only ordinary intelligence. That book has so much that is similar to things they do accept that it seems to me to be great stupidity not to accept this too, and, if there is anything there that upsets them, to say that that is untrue and an insertion. If this kind of talk is shameful, as it is, why do they think it has any validity in relation to Paul's epistles, and why do they think that it has any validity in relation to the four books of the gospel? I would venture to say that in these books there is proportionately much more that they would have us believe was inserted by corruptors of the text than there is in that book.

---

16. The passages rejected as forgeries were those that contradicted the teaching of Mani. Among them were the infancy narratives with their story of Davidic descent, birth, circumcision, and then the baptism, all of which show Jesus to be a true human being with a fleshly body and connect him with Judaism. Also rejected were all positive references to the Old Testament in the discourses of Jesus and his disciples. Faustus the Manichean explained such texts thus: unknown authors who wrote the gospels long after the time of Jesus and the disciples were impelled on behalf of the Jews to insert false information into the accounts in question. See *Confessions* V, 11, 21.

That is certainly how it seems to me. I ask you to think about this with me, assessing it calmly and without anxiety. You know that, in their attempt to count their founder Mani personally as one of the apostles,[17] they say that the Holy Spirit, whom the Lord promised to send to his disciples, came to us through him.[18] If they accepted those Acts of the Apostles, where the coming of the Holy Spirit is clearly preached,[19] there is no way they could maintain that that was an interpolation. They would have it that certain corruptors of the sacred books existed before the time of Mani himself and that they corrupted those books because they wanted to associate the law of the Jews with the gospel. They cannot say this concerning the Holy Spirit, unless perhaps they say they foresaw what would be brought up against Mani at a future time, when he said that the Holy Spirit was sent through him, and they put that in their books. We shall have a fuller discussion of the Holy Spirit, however, on another occasion. For the present let us return to what I set out to do.

8. That the New Testament contains Old Testament history, explanation and analogy has been shown, I think, clearly enough. It remains to show what there is of allegory. In the gospel our redeemer himself makes use of allegory from the Old Testament when he says, *This generation asks for a sign; but they will not be given any sign except that of the prophet Jonah. Just as Jonah was in the belly of a whale for three days and three nights, so too the Son of Man will be in the heart of the earth for three days and three nights.* (Mt 12:39-40) And what shall I say about the apostle Paul? In the first epistle to the Corinthians he points out that even the actual history of the Exodus was symbolic of the future Christian people: *I would not have you unaware, brothers, that our ancestors were all under the cloud and all passed across*

---

17. What is described here was not, however, a subordination but the relationship of a precursor to a successor who was greater than he. See the Cologne Mani Codex 66, 4-5 (L. Koenen and C. Römer, eds., *Papyrologica Coloniensia* 14 [Opladen 1988]); *Epistula fundamenti*, frag. 1 (E. Feldmann, ed. [Altenberge 1987]); L. Koenen, "Augustine and Manicheeism in Light of the Cologne Mani Codex, *Illinois Classical Studies* 3 (1978) 154-195, esp. 167-168.

18. See *Answer to Adimantus, a Disciple of Mani* 17; *Answer to Faustus, a Manichean* XIX, 31; *Answer to Felix, a Manichean* 1,2-5. See also Koenen, "Augustine and Manicheeism in Light of the Cologne Mani Codex" 168-176.

19. See Acts 2.

the sea. In the cloud and the sea they were all baptized for Moses; all ate the same spiritual food, and all drank the same spiritual drink; for they drank from the spiritual rock that followed them; and that rock was Christ. With most of them, however, God was not well pleased, and they were struck down in the desert. These things were an image for us, to warn us not to yearn for evil as they yearned for it. We must not worship idols, as they did (as the Scripture says, The people sat down to eat and drink and got up to play). We must not commit adultery, as some of them committed adultery, and twenty-three thousand fell on one day. We must not put Christ to the test, as some of them put him to the test, and they were killed by snakes. We must not complain, as some of them complained and were wiped out by the Destroyer. All this happened to them as a sign; and it was written down as a warning for us, for whom the last age has arrived. (1 Cor 10:1-11)

The apostle also has another allegory, although certainly relating mainly to causes. They themselves often referred to it and expounded it in their own arguments. It is what Paul says to the Galatians: *It is written that Abraham had two sons, one from a slave and one from a free woman; but the one from the slave was born by the flesh, whereas the one from the free woman was born as the result of a promise. These things are said as an allegory. The women are the two testaments. One is from Mount Sinai and her children are born into slavery; and that one is Hagar, as Mount Sinai is a mountain in Arabia. She corresponds to the present Jerusalem, which is in slavery along with her children. The Jerusalem above is the free woman, and she is the mother of us all.* (Gal 4:22-26)

9. Those people do little harm by this. In trying to invalidate the law, they force us to justify that scripture. They note that it says that we are slaves, and they brandish above the rest the concluding words, *You who are justified in the law are emptied of Christ; you have fallen from grace* (Gal 5:4). We acknowledge the truth of all this, and we do not say the law is necessary except for those who still benefit from being slaves. It was good for the law to be in effect, because men and women who could not be persuaded from sinning by reason had to be constrained by a law like that, that is to say, by the threat and dread of those punishments, which even the

foolish can apprehend. When Christ's grace sets us free from this, it does not condemn that law, but the time comes when he invites us to submit to his love and not be slaves to the law from fear. This is the grace, in other words, the benefit, that those who still yearn to be in bondage to the law fail to perceive as coming from God. Paul rightly castigates them as unbelievers, because they do not believe that through our Lord Jesus Christ they have now been set free from the slavery in which, by God's most just plan, they were held subject for a set time. This explains that other text of the same apostle, *The law was our tutor in Christ* (Gal 3:24). So the one who later gave men and women a teacher to love first gave them a tutor to fear. Although it is wrong now for Christians to observe those precepts and commandments of the law, such as the Sabbath and circumcision and sacrifices and the like, there is still much symbolism in them. Any devout person, therefore, understands that there is nothing more harmful than to take everything there according to the literal meaning of the words but that there is nothing more beneficial than to have it unveiled by the Spirit. So it is that *the letter kills but the spirit gives life* (2 Cor 3:6);[20] and so it is that *in the reading of the Old Testament the veil itself remains, and the veil is not lifted, because it is taken away with Christ* (2 Cor 3:14). It is not the Old Testament that is taken away with Christ, but the veil over it. What is dark and hidden without Christ is understood, and as it were uncovered, through Christ. The same apostle immediately adds, *When, however, you go over to Christ, the veil will be taken away* (2 Cor 3:16). He does not say that the law or the Old Testament will be taken away. So it is not that they have been taken away through the Lord's grace, because there is nothing good hidden there, but rather the cover that hides the good things there has been taken away.

This is what happens for those who are earnest and devout in searching for the meaning of those writings, and not undisciplined and ill-intentioned. They are shown how things are related to each other, and the reasons behind what was said and done, and the

---

20. In *Revisions* I, 14, 1 Augustine says that he gave a better interpretation of this verse from Galatians in *The Spirit and the Letter* 4, 6-5, 8, but he does not retract the interpretation given here.

harmony of the Old Testament and the New, which is so complete that there remains no point of disharmony, and the deep secrets of the figurative meaning. Everything the interpretation extracts forces us to recognize the wretchedness of those who choose to condemn these sources before learning about them.

4, 10. Leaving aside deep scholarship for the moment, let me deal with you in the way I think I should deal with someone close to me, and do what I am able to do rather than what I admired the most learned men for being able to do. There are three kinds of error that lead people astray when they read anything, and I shall say something about each of them. The first is what occurs when something untrue is taken to be the truth, although it is not what the writer thought. The second is not so widespread, but it is no less damaging: this occurs when something is taken to be the truth, and it is because it is also what the writer thought. The third kind of error occurs when something true is understood from the writings of others, although the authors did not have that understanding of it themselves. There is no small benefit to be gained from this. In fact, if you think carefully about it, that is the entire benefit of reading.

It would be an example of the first kind of error if someone said and believed, for instance, that in the underworld Rhadamanthus hears the cases of the dead and pronounces judgment on them, as that is what one reads in Virgil's poem.[21] Here there is a twofold error, because one believes something it is wrong to believe, and it is also wrong to think that the writer believed it.

The second kind of error is exemplified by someone who decides it is true and has to be believed that the soul is made up of atoms and that after death it breaks up into those atoms and passes away, because this is what Lucretius wrote.[22] This person is no less wretched for being convinced in a matter of such importance that something untrue is proven, even though that was the view of Lucretius, the writer of the books that caused the deception. What is gained from knowing for certain what the author thought, when one is choosing to be wrong with him rather than wrong because of him?

---

21. See *Aeneid* VI, 566ff.
22. See *De rerum natura* III, 231-257; 323-349; 425-426; 437-712; 830-930.

An example of the third kind of error would be the case of someone who reads a passage in Epicurus' writings, where he praises abstinence, and then asserts that Epicurus held virtue to be mankind's supreme good and that therefore he should not be criticized. If in fact Epicurus holds that bodily pleasure is mankind's supreme good, what harm comes from that person's mistake, since there is no acceptance of that immoral and dangerous doctrine and no approval of Epicurus on any other count? The only harm is in thinking he did not hold wrong views. This is not only human error but is often a very honorable human error. Why so? Suppose that it was reported to me about someone I loved that, even though he was a grown man, he said in the hearing of many people that he found childhood and infancy pleasant, even to the point of saying on oath that that is how he wanted to live; and suppose I was given such proof of this that I could not honorably deny it. Suppose, however, that I concluded that, when he said that, he only meant that he preferred innocence and a mind foreign to those desires that enmesh the human race, and because of this I loved him even more than I had before, even though perhaps he had also been foolishly infatuated with a certain freedom to play and eat and with the indolent idleness of childhood? Would anyone think I should be blamed for this? Suppose then that he died after I heard this report, and there was no one I could question to clarify what he thought. Would anyone be so shameless as to censure me for praising the intentions and desires I inferred from the actual words reported to me? Indeed, a fair judge of the matter would not hesitate perhaps even to praise my thinking and attitude because I not only approved of innocence but also, when there was doubt about the facts, preferred to think well of a fellow human being, even when it would not be wrong to think evil.

5, 11. This being the case, attend as well to the corresponding differences in the status of those writings. There has to be the same number of possibilities. Either someone wrote something worthwhile, but there is nothing worthwhile in someone's understanding of it; or there is nothing of value in either case; or there is benefit for a reader who understands it in a way contrary to what the author wrote. Of these three alternatives, I have nothing against the first, and I am not concerned about the last. I cannot criticize any writers who are misunderstood through no fault of their own. Nor can I take it badly that someone who fails to see the truth is read, when I see that no harm is done to the reader.

The one case that is fully approvable and as it were unblemished occurs when what is written is good and is also taken by readers to their advantage. Even this can still be distinguished as occurring in two ways, for the possibility of error is not entirely excluded. It usually happens that, when the writer has perceived well, the reader perceives well too, but the reader perceives differently from the author, often better, often worse, but always for good. And so, when we perceive what the author we are reading perceived—and it is something very relevant to leading a good life—truth is piled on truth and there is no opening left for falsehood. When the reading is about very obscure matters this case is entirely rare, and in my opinion it cannot be known for sure but can only be believed to occur. By what arguments can I conclude, so as to be able to swear to it, what the intentions were of persons who are dead or absent? Even if they were available for questioning, there could be much that good persons would have to conceal. For the purpose of discovering the truth, however, I do not think it matters what kind of person the author was. The honorable way is to assume that anyone whose writings serve the interests of the human race and future generations was a good person.

12. For these reasons I wish these people would tell me which kind of error they think the Catholic Church makes. If it is the first, then it is a very serious allegation but not one that requires an extended defense. It is enough to say that we do not understand it in the way they ascribe to us in their attack. If it is the second kind of error, it is no less serious, but they are refuted with the same statement. If it is the third, there is nothing to answer.

Let them go ahead and look at the scriptures themselves. What is their objection with regard to the books that are called the Old Testament? Can it be that they are good but that we interpret them badly? But they themselves do not accept them. Or is it that they are not good and that the way we take them is bad? The answer above is enough to refute this. Or do they say this: "Although your response to them is good, they themselves are bad"? What else is this but to exonerate the living opponents with whom they are now dealing and to blame the dead with whom they have no argument?

I myself believe that those writers did well in putting everything on record, and that they were great and divinely inspired, and that that law was established and promulgated at God's command and according to his wishes. Although my knowledge of those books is very limited, I can easily prove this to anyone who listens to me with an open mind, free of obstinacy. Since we have the resources of your well-intentioned ears and mind, I shall do this, but I shall do it when I have the opportunity. Is it not enough for the present that, whatever the facts in that regard, I have not been deceived?

6. 13. My own conscience, Honoratus, and the God who dwells in pure souls are my witness that in my estimation there is nothing wiser or purer or more sacred than all those writings that the Catholic Church preserves under the name of the Old Testament. This, I know, surprises you. I cannot pretend that I was not once convinced quite to the contrary. But with any books there is nothing more full of that brashness which possessed us then as children than to abandon the instructors who claim they understand and accept them and can pass them on to their pupils and look to discover their meaning from those who, for whatever compelling reason, have declared bitter war on their authors and publishers. Who ever thought to have the learned and difficult works of Aristotle[23] expounded by his enemies, to speak of studies where the reader may well make a slip without committing sacrilege? Or who has ever chosen to read and learn the geometry of Archimedes with Epicurus as tutor? In many of his writings he opposed them tenaciously, although, in my opinion, without understanding them at all. Are those scriptures of the law, that they attack so foolishly and so ineffectually as though they were open to all, entirely transparent? They seem to me to be like that simple woman whom they themselves often hold up to ridicule,

---

23. Augustine knew the *Categories* of Aristotle from having read it himself (see *Confessions* IV, 16, 28), probably in the translation of Marius Victorinus. Otherwise he had only a limited and mainly indirect knowledge of Aristotle's works.

who became angry because a certain Manichean woman praised the sun and commended it to her for worship.[24] Religiously naive, she jumped up excitedly and repeatedly stamped on the spot that shone in the sunlight from the window. "See, I stamp on your sun and your god," she began to shout. It was her woman's way and quite foolish of her—who would say otherwise? But do you not think they too are just the same when, with a massive onslaught of speeches and curses, they tear at things they do not understand? They have no understanding of their nature or purpose, or how they are like ruins, although they are subtle and divine for those who understand them. Because the ignorant applaud them, they think they have achieved something.

Believe me, everything in that scripture is profound and from God. There is absolute truth there, and teaching finely adapted to the renewal and restoration of souls and clearly presented in such a way that there is no one who cannot draw from it. This is all anyone needs, provided he comes to draw from it in a spirit of devout respect, as true religion requires. To prove this for you would require considerable reasoning and a longer discourse. We must first do what we have to do for you. We must ensure that you do not despise the actual authors and then bring you to love them. How is this to be done other than by an exposition of their own statements and writings? If we had hated Virgil, before we understood him, or even if we did not love him because of the approval of our ancestors, we would never be satisfied with regard to those countless questions about him that keep grammarians busy and excited. We would not be content to listen to someone who explained them favorably to him, but we would prefer someone who tried to use them to show that he was wrong and deluded. As it is, however, many try to elucidate them, according to their own different interpretations, and the greatest applause is accorded to those whose commentary makes him the more excellent poet. Even those who do not understand him believe not only that he did nothing badly but also that he wrote no poetry that was not praiseworthy. Therefore, when our teachers fail us and do not have an answer on some questions of

---

24. The Manicheans venerated the sun as a "ship of light" that gathered up the portions of light that had been liberated from matter and carried them onward. See *Heresies* 46, 6.

detail, rather than thinking their silence might be accounted for by some defect in Virgil, we become resentful. If in their own justification they choose to find fault with such a great author, hardly any of their pupils will stay with them, even if paid to.

How important was it for us to extend the same good will to those through whom, as such a long tradition assures us, the Holy Spirit spoke? We, however (brilliant young men and wonderful researchers of reason that we were!), without even opening those writings, and without looking for teachers, and in no danger of being accused of tardiness, did not give even passing attention to those who throughout the whole world have for so long sought to have those documents read and preserved and handed on. Yet we concluded there was nothing in them worth believing. Excited by the speech of those who were enemies and hostile to them, we were persuaded by their false promise of proofs to accept and cultivate an incredible number of myths.[25]

7, 14. Now, if I can, let me complete what I began. My purpose with you is not just to reveal the Catholic faith in passing but to open up for those who have a care for their own souls the hope of a divine outcome and the discovery of truth. No one doubts that anyone who is looking for the true religion either believes already that the soul is immortal and that that religion is for its good, or he at least wants to find that out in that religion. The soul, therefore, is the reason for all religion. Whatever the nature of the body, it excites no concern or anxiety, especially after death, for anyone who is intent on the soul and its happiness. If there is a true religion, it is either for the soul alone or principally for the soul that it was founded. As we know, however, this soul is foolish and makes mistakes (I shall look into the reason for this, and I admit it is very obscure), until it attains and apprehends wisdom, and perhaps that itself is the true religion.

Would I direct you to myths? Would I force you to believe something wrongly? I say that our soul is trapped and immersed in error and stupidity and is looking for the way of truth, if there is one. If that is not how it is with you, then forgive me and please share your wisdom with me. But if you do recognize the truth of

---

25. The Manicheans demanded the very thing for which they criticized the Catholic Church.

what I am saying in yourself, then, I implore you, let us look for the truth together.

15. Suppose that we had not yet heard anyone preaching any religion. It is still something new to us, an activity just begun. If there is anything in it at all, I think we have to look for teachers in the subject. Suppose that we find there are different ones, each holding different views and all wanting to attract everyone to themselves with their different views. Among them, however, some stand out because of their greater present reputation and the almost universal attention they receive. The important question is whether they have the truth. But must we not investigate them first, so that if we do go wrong, human as we are, we might seem to go wrong along with the whole human race?

16. Some few have the truth. If you know who has it, you already know what it is. Did I not just say to you that we would search as though we knew nothing? But if truth itself forces you to conclude that only a few have it, yet you do not know who those few are, what then? If those who know the truth, so as to be able to hold the masses by their authority, are so few in number, how is it that those few are able to extricate themselves, and be purified, as it were, to enter those secret places? Do we not see how few there are who attain perfect eloquence, even though throughout the whole world schools of oratory resound to the clatter of the flocks of young students? Does it happen that anyone who wants to become a good speaker is frightened away by the untalented masses and decides to concentrate on the speeches of Caecilius or Erucus[26] rather than those of Cicero? These are supported by the authority of our ancestors, and everyone looks to them. The untalented crowd set out to study the same speeches as the few learned pupils are given to study. Very few get started, however; fewer still complete the task; and only a tiny number excel. What if the true religion is like that? What if great masses of the uneducated attend the churches, though beyond question this does not result in anyone's being made perfect by those rites?

26. The reference is to two opponents in famous trials. Q. Caecilius Niger claimed for himself, instead of Cicero, the right to prosecute Verres, but Cicero in his *Divinatio in Caecilium* eliminated him as unfit because he was an accomplice of Verres. C. Erucus was the prosecutor of Sextus Roscius from America, whom Cicero successfully defended.

If the number who studied oratory were as few as the number who are eloquent, our parents would never have thought to send us to those teachers. Since, therefore, we were attracted to those studies by the numbers of mostly uneducated persons, and as a result we grew to love something that few manage to attain, why do we not want it to be the same for us in the case of religion? Why do we perhaps hold it in contempt for being like that, to the great peril of our soul? It may be that true and genuine worship of God resides only with a few people, but it nevertheless does reside with them; and it may be that the masses agree with them, even though they are tied down by their desires and cut off from intellectual purity—and who has any doubt that this can happen? If, then, I ask you, anyone accuses us of being reckless and irrational because we do not carefully investigate the religion we are so concerned to discover in the works of its masters, what answer can we give? Have the masses frightened me away? Why is it that the masses have not frightened me away from the study of the liberal arts,[27] which scarcely contribute anything useful even to this present life? Why have they not frightened me away from the quest for money? Why have they not frightened me away from the pursuit of honor? Why have they not frightened me away from acquiring and maintaining good health? And finally, why have they not frightened me away even from the desire of a happy life? These are things everyone works for and in which few achieve excellence.

17. These would seem to be absurd things to say. Who would make such statements? Only enemies. Whatever the cause, and whatever the reason—and I am not investigating this now—they are enemies. I found this out for myself when I read them. Is that how it is? If you had no literary education you would not dare to open Terence Maurus[28] without a teacher. To learn to understand any poet, even one whose poetry is seen to win the applause of

----

27. See *Order* II, 12, 35: grammar, rhetoric, dialectic, music, geometry, astronomy, and arithmetic. According to *Revisions* I, 3, this is the sequence of studies "whereby one can advance from corporeal realities to incorporeal ones."

28. A Latin grammarian from Africa in the second/third century A.D. He composed didactic poems, the content of which dealt with the theory of language.

the theatre, Asper, Cornutus, Donatus[29] and countless others are consulted. So, do you rush in without a guide and, without a teacher, dare to pass judgment on those books that, whatever else there may be about them, are widely acknowledged by almost the entire human race to be holy and full of divine content? If you find something in them that seems absurd, do you not find fault with yourself for being slow and having a mind polluted by the poison of this world,[30] the same as all foolish people, rather than finding fault with those who perhaps cannot be understood by minds like that? Would you not look for someone both holy and learned, or at least having that reputation among many people, to instruct and teach you, in order to become both a better person and more learned? Would it be easy to find someone like that, even if you searched hard? Was there no one like that in the region where you lived? What better reason could you have to force you to travel? Was there no one like that, or you could find no one like that, on the continent? Then you would set sail. If you found no one like that in the nearest land across the sea, you would travel on, as far as the lands in which the events contained in those books are said to have occurred. Did we do anything like that, Honoratus? Yet, pitiful youngsters that we were, by our own judgment and assessment we condemned what was perhaps (I speak as though there were still some doubt about it) the most sacred religion, and one that was already respected throughout the whole world. What if certain things there seemed to be harmful for people who had no expertise in those scriptures? Could it be that they were put there so that, when we read things that were repulsive not only to the sensibility of the wise and holy but to the sensibilities of people generally, we would look much more carefully for the hidden meaning? Do you not notice how people try to interpret the Ganymede of the *Bucolics*, when he turns out to be a cruel shepherd, and the boy

---

29. Latin grammarians. Aemilius Asper lived in the second century A.D. "Cornutus" probably refers to L. Annaeus Cornutus (first century A.D.), who was a Stoic philosopher as well as a teacher of the poets Persius and Lucan. Donatus Aelius lived in the middle of the fourth century A.D. All three authors composed commentaries on Virgil.
30. See *The Magnitude of the Soul* 33, 74.

Alexis,[31] to whom it is said that Plato also wrote a love song?[32] They interpret it as having some deep symbolic meaning,[33] which they say escapes the perception of the uneducated, even though it would be no sacrilege to think that the prolific poet also composed some sensual verses.

18. What in fact drew us back and kept us from investigating it? Was it the threat of some law, or the strength of its opponents, or the foul character or evil reputation of the consecrated ministers, or the novelty of the teaching, or the secrecy of the membership? It was none of these things. Every divine and human law allows inquiry into the Catholic faith. Under human law it is certainly lawful to accept it and foster it,[34] even if, as long as we are in error about it, there may be some doubt about the divine law. There is no enemy striking fear into us in our frailty. (Even so, if truth and the soul's salvation are not found after careful inquiry where it is lawful and safe, it ought to be sought at any risk.) Every level of honor and authority is committed to the service of this divine worship. Religion has the highest standing and honor. What is there then to prevent examination and discussion, with a devout and careful investigation, as to whether we have here that thing which only a few need know and preserve with full understanding, even though it has the united approval and acceptance of all nations?

19. With this understanding let us proceed now in the way that I said. First we must ask what religion we shall commit our souls to for cleansing and renewal. Without question we must begin with the Catholic Church. There are now more Christians than even pagans and Jews combined. Although there are numerous heresies among those Christians, and all want to be seen as Catholics and they call those other than themselves heretics, everyone agrees that there is only one Church. Taking into account the whole world, it

---

31. See Virgil, *Eclogue* 2.
32. See Apuleius, *Apologia* 10; Diogenes Laertius, *Lives and Opinions of the Philosophers* III, 23, 31.
33. Augustine's knowledge of the allegorical interpretation of Virgil must have come from his study of rhetoric. Thus he was familiar with the method of allegorical interpretation before he learned from Ambrose how to apply it to the Bible. See J. Stroux, "Zur allegorischen Deutung Virgils," *Philologus* 86 (1931) 363-368.
34. After the edict *Cunctos populos* (380) of Emperor Theodosius the Catholic faith was even the legally prescribed religion of the Roman state.

has the greatest numbers. Also, as those who know assert, it is more sincere about the truth than all the rest. Truth, however, is another question. For the one who is investigating that is enough. There is one Catholic Church, although different heresies give it different names, because each of them has its own name that it does not dare to reject. Consequently it is left to the judgment of those who assess it unhampered by any special interest to judge which one should be accorded the name of Catholic to which all aspire. In case anyone thinks there has to be a lengthy, wordy discussion on this point, there is no dispute that it is one Church only, and in a certain way even human laws are Christian in it.

I do not want any prejudgment to be drawn from this; but I think it is the most appropriate starting point for our inquiry. We must not have any fear that the true worship of God might seem to need propping up by those who in fact need it for their own support, rather than standing by its own strength. Undoubtedly the ideal is for the truth to be able to be discovered where it can be investigated and retained in perfect security; but, if this is not possible, then other sources must be approached and explored, whatever the perils.

8, 20. Having made these points, which in my opinion are so right that I ought to win your verdict against any opponent, I shall outline for you as best I can the path I followed when I was searching for the true religion, in the state of mind that I have just shown is the state of mind which that search requires.

When I left you to go across the sea,[35] I was already procrastinating and hesitating about what to hold and what to reject. This hesitancy grew stronger in me from the moment I heard that person who, as you know, we had been promised would come as though from heaven to explain everything that troubled us.[36] Apart from having a certain eloquence I found that he was just like the rest. I thought about it within myself, and, now settled in Italy, I struggled to decide not whether to stay in that sect that I regretted

---

35. The reference is to Augustine's leaving Carthage for Rome in 383; see *Confessions* V, 8, 14-15.
36. The reference is to the Manichean bishop Faustus of Milevis; see ibid. V, 6, 10 – 7, 13.

joining[37] but how to find the truth. No one knows my love and yearning for that better than yourself. Often it seemed to me that it could not be found, and I turned the great flood of my thoughts to the opinions of the academics.[38] Often, as best I could, I would look again at the human mind, so lively, so discerning, so perceptive, and I would think that the truth could not lie hidden unless the way to search for it lay hidden and that that way had itself to be obtained from some divine authority. It only remained to find out what authority that was, since among all their disagreements everyone promised to provide it.

So there was a bewildering forest, and it had finally become intolerable to be planted in it. At the same time the desire for truth continued to drive my mind on without respite. I had already decided to leave them, and I was becoming more and more convinced I should do so. In the midst of such great dangers there was nothing left for me except with tearful, piteous cries to implore divine providence to give me strength,[39] and I did that earnestly. Already some arguments of the Bishop of Milan had almost persuaded me that it would not be unproductive if I chose to look at a large number of matters concerning the Old Testament which, as you know, we blasphemed against because they were misrepresented to us. I had also decided to be a catechumen in the Church to which I had been presented by my parents, for as long as it took either to find what I wanted or to become convinced it was not to be found.[40] At that time, therefore, anyone able to teach me would have found me ready and very receptive.

Your soul should be in a similar state of concern now. You too are aware that you have been unsettled for a long time. If you now think you have been tossed around enough and want to put an end to these struggles, then follow the path of the Catholic teaching, which has flowed down to us from Christ himself through his apostles and will continue to flow down to our descendants.

---

37. But even in Rome Augustine had contacts with the Manicheans; see ibid. V, 10, 18 – 11, 21; 13, 23.
38. Augustine was drawing closer to philosophical skepticism. The so-called New Academy held the view that the mind could at best reach probable knowledge.
39. This came through Ambrose, who had a decisive influence on Augustine, especially through his sermons in the spring of 386.
40. See *Confessions* V, 14, 25.

9, 21. "That is absurd," you say, "because this is what everyone claims to hold and teach." I cannot deny that all the heretics make this claim. They do so, however, by promising those they seduce that they will provide understanding of the most obscure matters, and by accusing the Catholic teaching especially for its insistence that those who come to it must have belief. They themselves boast that they do not impose a yoke of belief but open up a fountain of doctrine.[41] "What can we say to this," you ask, "because it redounds so much to their credit?" That is not how it is. They do not do this because of any ability they have, but to attract numbers in the name of reason. The human spirit is naturally delighted by that promise, and without considering its own strength and state of health, but hungering after the food of the strong, harmful though it is for anyone unhealthy, it rushes on to the deceivers' poison. There is no right way of entering into the true religion without believing things that all who live rightly and become worthy of it will understand and see for themselves later on, and without some submission to a certain weight of authority.

22. Perhaps you want to be given some proof of this as well, to convince you that you do not have to learn by reason before being taught by faith.[42] This is not hard to do, provided you keep an open mind. To make it easier, I want you to answer as though someone were questioning you. First of all, tell me why you think one should not believe. "Because," you say, "credulity itself, from which those who are called credulous get their name, seems to me to be a defect. Otherwise we would not commonly use this term as a criticism. If being suspicious is a fault, in that one suspects something not proven, how much more is it a fault to be credulous. The only difference between this and being suspicious is that the suspicious person has some doubt about things that are not known, whereas the credulous person has none."

I will accept this opinion and distinction for the present, but you also know that we do not usually call someone curious without some element of criticism, but we call someone studious even as

41. See *ibid*. VI, 5, 7; Letter 118, 5, 32.
42. For the line of argument that follows see Letter 120, 1, 3.

a compliment. Consider, therefore, if you will, what you think is the difference between these two. You will answer for sure that, although both are motivated by a strong desire for knowledge, the curious ask about things that are none of their business, whereas the studious inquire about things relating to themselves. Yet we do not deny that one's own spouse and children and their well-being are important for everyone, and when those who are away from home question in detail everyone who comes to them as to how their spouses and children are keeping and what they are doing, they are driven by an intense desire to know; but we do not call them studious. It is true that anyone who is studious wants to know about things relating to themselves. It is not true, however, that everyone who does that should be called studious but only those who spend themselves inquiring about what relates to the finer nourishment and adornment of the mind.[43] At the same time it is correct to say they are keen to know, especially if we add what it is they are keen to know about. We might even call them studious about their own family, if they only care about their own family, even if we do not think they deserve the general name of studious without qualification. We would not call those who wanted to hear about their own family studious, unless they enjoyed a good reputation and they wanted to hear it often; but we would call them keen to know, even if it was only once.

Now turn your attention again to the curious person and tell me: if someone listened willingly to stories that brought no benefit at all to himself, that is, about things not relating to himself, yet did not do so as a habit and maliciously but only rarely and with restraint, either at a dinner or in some meeting or gathering, would you say that person was curious? I do not think so. On the other hand you would certainly think that about someone who listened freely because he took such things seriously. So the definition of a curious person has to be qualified by the same restriction as that of the studious person. See, therefore, whether what was said previously has to be corrected. Why would it not be both that a person who sometimes suspects something does not deserve to be called suspicious and that a person who sometimes believes

---

43. The reference is to the liberal arts; see section 16.

something does not deserve to be called credulous? Therefore, just as there is a great difference between being keen to know something and being simply studious, and between being interested in something and being curious, so too there is a great difference between believing and being credulous.

10, 23. "Just the same," you say, "see now whether we ought to believe in matters of religion. If we agree that believing something is not the same as being credulous, it does not follow that there is nothing wrong with believing something in matters of religion. What if believing and being credulous are both wrong, just as being drunk and being a drunkard are?" If anyone thinks this is beyond question, I do not think he can have any friends.[44] If it is wrong to believe anything, then either one does wrong by believing a friend or one never believes a friend, and then I do not see how one can call either oneself or the friend a friend. Perhaps you will say to this, "I grant that we should believe something sometimes, but show me now how it is not wrong to believe without knowing in matters of religion." I shall do that, if I can; and to that end I ask you, "Which do you think is the more serious fault, handing religion on to someone unworthy of it or believing what is said by those who hand it on?" If you do not understand what I mean by someone unworthy, it is someone who comes with a feigned interest. You will agree, I think, that one is more to be blamed for revealing holy secrets, if there are any, to someone like that than for believing the representatives of a religion when they make statements about that religion. It would be unworthy of you to answer otherwise. So, now imagine there is someone present who is going to hand that religion on to you. How will you assure that person that you come with a sincere mind and that you have no deceit or pretence in this respect? You will say in good conscience that you are not pretending anything and will assert this with the best words possible, but still only with words. You cannot reveal the hidden recesses of your mind to another human being, to be known from within. If the person then says, "Look, I believe you. So isn't it fair that

---

44. See *Faith in the Unseen* 1, 2.

you also should believe me, since, if I have any truth, it is you who are going to receive the benefit and I who am going to bestow it?" What answer shall we give, other than that we should believe?

24. "But," you say, "would it not be better if you gave me proof, so that in following you wherever you lead me I would do nothing irrational?" Perhaps so, but since it is so important for you to know God by reason, do you think everyone is capable of grasping the arguments that lead the human mind to divine understanding? Or do you think most people are capable of it? Or only a few? "Only a few," I think you will say. Do you think you are one of these? "That is not for me to answer," you say. So you think it is for the other person to believe this about you too; and this is what happens. Remember then that the other person has now believed you on two occasions when you have said something unsubstantiated, although your religious advice is not to consent to believe even once. Let us grant, however, that you are sincere in your approach to accepting the religion and that you are one of the few who can understand the reasoning by which the divine faculty is brought to certain knowledge. What then? Do you think religion has to be denied to the rest of mankind, who are not endowed with such a clear intellect? Or do you think they have to be introduced to those deep secrets gradually and in stages? You can see clearly what is more truly religious. You cannot think that anyone who longs for something so important should be abandoned or rejected in any way. Do you not see, though, that, unless they believe they will achieve what they set out for and come to it with a suppliant mind, purified by a particular way of living in obedience to certain important, essential commandments, there is no other way for them to attain those perfect truths? You surely believe that.

So, what about those (among whom I think you would be included) who are easily able to grasp the divine secrets with sure reasoning. If they receive them in the same way as those who at first only believe, do you think this will do them any harm? I do not think so. "Just the same," you say, "why do they need to wait?" Because, although it does them no harm at all to wait, their example would be harmful to others. There is hardly anyone who has a true opinion of himself. Those who underestimate themselves need to be encouraged, those who overestimate themselves need to be repressed, so that the former will not break with despair and the latter will not crash through overconfidence. This is easily effected if even those who can fly are made to proceed gradually, in a way that is safe for the others too, and so that no one is incited to take risks. This is the wisdom of the true religion. This is the divine command. This is the tradition of our holy ancestors. This has been the practice until now. To choose to disturb and distort this is nothing other than to look for the true religion along a path of sacrilege. Even if they are allowed to act as they wish, those who act in this way cannot reach their goal. They may be as brilliant as you like, but if God is not with them they crawl along on the ground. God, however, is with those who seek him with care for humanity. There cannot be found any more secure path to heaven than this.

I for my part certainly cannot oppose this argument, for who can say we should believe nothing that we do not know for certain? Even friendship cannot exist unless we believe some things that cannot be proved for certain. The servants in charge of expenditure are often believed without any fault on the part of their master. In religion what could be more wicked than for God's bishops to believe us when we avow our sincerity, while we refuse to believe them when they instruct us? Finally, what more salutary way can there be than first of all to be made fit to perceive the truth by accepting on faith the things that have been instituted by God to prepare and predispose the mind, or, if you are already perfectly prepared, to circle for a while where the approach is safest rather than to be a cause of danger to yourself and an example of reck-lessness to others?

11, 25. It remains now to consider the reasons why it is wrong to follow those who promise to lead us by reason. We have already shown how there is nothing wrong with following those who insist that we believe. There are some who think not only that they should not be blamed for turning to those patrons of reason but even that they should be praised for it. Not so. In relation to religion there are two kinds of persons who deserve to be praised. The first is those who have already found it, and they must be considered the happiest; the other is those who are dedicated to the proper search for it. The first have already arrived, while the others are on the path by which they will surely arrive.[45]

There are three other kinds of persons who undoubtedly deserve blame and contempt. The first is the opinionated ones, that is, those who think they know what they do not know. The second is those who are aware that they do not know but do not use the right methods to find out. The third is those who do not think they know nor want to find out. In the human mind too there are three very closely related things that it is very important to distinguish: understanding, believing, and being opinionated. Considered in themselves, the first is always good; the second is sometimes wrong, and the third is never without fault. To understand things that are important and good, or even divine, is the happiest thing.[46] To understand inessential things does no harm, although learning about them could be harmful by taking up the time needed for essential things. To understand things that are bad for us is no misfortune, but to do them or endure them is. If someone understands how to kill an enemy without risk, the actual understanding does not have the guilt of the desire to do it. If that is not there, what could be more innocent? Believing, however, is at fault on those occasions when something unfitting is believed about God or too easily believed about another person. In other matters there is nothing wrong with believing, provided one understands it is something one does not know. I believe that criminal conspirators were once executed through the influence of Cicero,[47] but not only do I not know it, but I know for certain that there is no way I can know it. To be opinionated, however, is bad for two reasons. Those who are already convinced they know something are not able to learn about it, if learning about it becomes possible, and being hasty is in itself a sign of an ill-adjusted mind. If anyone thinks that he has knowledge about the subject I mentioned concerning

---

45. In his later years Augustine was convinced that complete happiness could only be found in the life after death, because only then would the truth, that is, God, be fully known; see *Revisions* I, 14, 2.
46. In *Revisions* I, 14, 2 Augustine again stresses the point that this statement must be referred to happiness in the life to come.
47. This is an allusion to the Catiline plot of 63 B.C.

Cicero, this is no hindrance at all to his acquiring knowledge of it, since it is not a matter about which it is possible to have knowledge. Nevertheless they do not understand that it matters a great deal whether something is ascertained by the secure mental reasoning that we call understanding, or whether for good reasons it is entrusted to oral tradition and writing for the belief of future generations. In this they are certainly making a mistake, and there is no mistake that does not have something bad about it.

Therefore, we must hold what we understand as coming from reason, what we believe as coming from authority,[48] and what we are opinionated about as coming from error. Anyone who understands also believes, and anyone who is opinionated also believes, but someone who believes does not always understand, and someone who is opinionated never understands.[49]

We can relate these three things to those five types of persons that we mentioned previously, namely, the two commendable ones that we mentioned first, and the other three that are reprehensible. We find that the first kind of person, the one who is happy, believes the truth itself, whereas the second, the keen lover of truth, believes authority; and in both these cases believing is commendable. With the first of the reprehensible ones, those who think they know what they do not know, there is certainly the fault of credulity. The other two reprehensible ones, those who seek the truth with no hope that they will find it[50] and those who do not seek it at all, do not believe anything. This moreover is in matters where there exists appropriate teaching. In other aspects of life I do not know how it is possible at all for someone not to believe anything. Even those who say they act according to probabilities[51] want to be seen as not able to know anything rather than as not believing anything. Does anyone test something without a belief about it? And how is the course

---

48. In *Revisions* I, 14, 3 Augustine points out that in everyday language, of which the Bible too makes use, "believe" and "know" are not so sharply distinguished from one another.

49. See *The Teacher* 11, 37, 2.

50. The supporters of philosophical skepticism must be meant.

51. Once again the reference is to the skeptics; see *Answer to the Skeptics* III, 1; *Confessions* VI, 11, 18.

he follows probable if it is not tested? Hence enemies of the truth can be of two kinds. There are those who only attack knowledge but do not attack belief; and there are those who condemn both. Whether people like this are actually to be found in human life once again I do not know.

I have said these things so that we might appreciate that in maintaining our belief in what we do not yet understand we are exonerated from the rashness of being opinionated. Anyone who says we should believe nothing that we do not know is only warning against what is called "being opinionated," and this admittedly is a miserable defect. If, however, he considers carefully the great difference there is between thinking one knows something and believing on authority something one is aware that one does not know, then he will surely avoid mistakes and escape the charge of being proud and lacking in humanity.

12, 26. If it is wrong to believe something we do not know, I should like to know how children can obey their parents and return their love and respect without believing they are their parents. There is no way this can be known by reason. We have a belief about our father based on the word of our mother. For our belief about our mother herself we usually depend not on our mother but on midwives, nurses and servants. Is it not possible for a mother to have her child stolen and another substituted for it and so, being deceived herself, to cause others to be deceived? We do believe, however, and believe without any hesitation, things that we admit we cannot know. Can anyone fail to see that, if this were not so, filial love, humanity's most sacred bond, would be the victim of criminal arrogance? Is there anyone even so insane as to blame those who carried out all the usual duties towards those they believed to be their parents, although they were not? Is there anyone on the other hand who would not condemn, as not fit to live, persons who failed to love their true parents for fear of loving impostors? There are many examples we could give to show that absolutely nothing in human society would be safe if we decided not to believe anything that we cannot hold as evident.[52]

---

52. See *Confessions* VI, 5, 7; *Faith in the Unseen* 2, 4. A similar view is expressed earlier in Cicero, *Laelius on Friendship* 7, 23.

27. Listen now to something about which I confess it will now be easier for me to persuade you. When we are dealing with religion, that is, worship and understanding of God, even less should we be guided by those who forbid us to believe and so freely promise us proofs.

No one will question that everyone is either foolish or wise.[53] By wise here I do not mean those who are wily and ingenious but those who have, as much as is possible for a human being, a strong perception and understanding both of human nature itself and of God and a way of life that conforms to this. All others, whatever their skills or lack of skills, and whatever their conquests in proving and disproving, I count among the foolish. If this is so, is there anyone of ordinary intelligence who does not see clearly that it is more effective and safer for the foolish to accept the guidance of the wise than to live according to their own judgment? Anything we do that is not done rightly is a sin, and nothing can be done rightly if it does not proceed from right reasoning. So right reasoning itself is a virtue. But where is this virtue present in humanity except in the minds of the wise? Only the wise, therefore, do not sin. All the foolish sin, except when they obey the wise. In that case what they do does proceed from right reasoning, and the foolish, so to speak, are not to be considered the owners of their own deeds, since they are like tools and agents of the wise. Therefore, if for everyone not sinning is better than sinning, the foolish would surely all live better lives if they could be the slaves of the wise. If no one questions the value of this in less important matters, such as commerce and farming, marrying, having and raising children, and the general management of the household, it is even more expedient in the case of religion. Not only are human affairs easier to assess than those that relate to God, but also, with anything of greater sanctity and excellence, the greater the respect and reverence due to it, the more wicked and perilous it is to sin.

---

53. In *Revisions* I, 14, 4 Augustine notes a seeming contradiction here to *Free Will* III, 24, 71, where a middle state between wisdom and ignorance is mentioned. But in that passage the reference is to two special cases—Adam before the Fall, and very little children.

It is clear that as long as we remain foolish, if we have our hearts set on leading a good and truly religious life, we have no alternative but to seek out the wise and be obedient to them. In this way, while the foolishness remains in us, we shall feel its domination less and one day be delivered from it.

13, 28. Here again there arises a very difficult question. How can the foolish find someone who is wise? Although hardly anyone would dare claim this title openly, most people would claim it for themselves indirectly. Because they disagree among themselves so much about the very things whose knowledge constitutes wisdom, it must be either that none of them is wise or that at the most one of them is. But who is that one? Since it is the foolish who are trying to find out, I do not see at all how they can distinguish clearly and discern who that one is. They cannot recognize something by any of its signs, if they have no knowledge of the thing itself whose presence they indicate.[54] It is not that someone who does not have it can discern wisdom with the mind's eye, in the way you are able to recognize gold and silver and things like that when you see them, even though you do not own any. Anything we apprehend with our bodily senses is presented to us externally, and so we can detect with our eyes things that belong to others, even when we ourselves have nothing the same or similar. What the intellect apprehends, however, is within the mind, and perceiving it is the same as having it. Since then the foolish do not have wisdom, and it is not possible for them to see it with their eyes, they do not know wisdom. It is not possible for them to perceive it without having it, and it is not possible for them to have it and be foolish. Therefore they do not know it, and as long as they do not know it they cannot recognize it anywhere else. So as long as one is foolish one cannot find with certainty the wise person to submit to in order to be delivered from that great evil of being foolish.

29. As our inquiry has to do with religion, the cure for this immense problem can only come from God, and, unless we believe both that he exists and that he can be invoked by the human mind,

---

54. See *The Teacher* 10, 33; *The Trinity* X, 1, 2.

we should not even look for the true religion. What are we trying to investigate with such great effort? What are we hoping to achieve? Where do we want to arrive? At some place that we do not believe exists or do not believe has any relevance for ourselves? Nothing could be more perverse than a mentality like that. You yourself would not venture to ask a favor from me, or would certainly be very stupid to do so, if you did not believe I would grant it. Do you come, then, asking to find out about religion, even though you think that God does not exist, or, if God does exist, that he does not care about us?

So then, what if it is something of such great importance but it cannot be discovered except by untiring investigation with all our resources? What if the extreme difficulty of the investigation itself trains the mind of the investigator to grasp and display the object it uncovers?[55] Is there anything more pleasant for our eyes or anything they are more at home with than light? Yet after a long period of darkness they cannot bear to endure it. For a body exhausted by illness is there anything more appropriate than food and drink? Yet we see people recovering from illness restrained and prevented from risking harm to themselves by eating fully as healthy people do. They are held back from using the food itself in such a way as to bring about a relapse into the illness that caused them to reject it. I am speaking of persons who are convalescing. What of those who are actually ill? Do we not encourage them to eat or drink something? And surely they would not obey us, when it is such an effort for them, if they did not believe they would recover from the illness.

When, therefore, would you commit yourself to a difficult and demanding inquiry? Would you ever dare to undertake such a heavy task and responsibility, matching the importance of its subject matter, if you did not believe that the object of your search existed? Rightly, therefore, has the high authority of the Catholic teaching made it the rule that, before all else, those coming to religion must be persuaded to have faith.

14, 30. I ask you, what arguments do those heretics put to me (since these people we are discussing want to be known as

---

55. See *Teaching Christianity* I on the interpretation of the Bible.

Christians)? How would they persuade me to abandon belief as
irrational? If they insist I should not believe anything, I do not
believe that in human life there is any true religion like this, and,
since I do not believe it exists, I do not search for it. He, however,
as I believe, is going to show it to anyone who searches: *Whoever
seeks, will find* (Mt 7:7).[56] Accordingly, I would not come to
someone who forbids me to believe unless I did believe something.
Could there be any greater insanity than this: they blame me only
because I have belief that is not supported by knowledge, although
it is only that which brought me to them?

31. What is this? The heretics all urge us not to believe
Christ. Could there be any greater self-contradiction? They
have to be pressed on this in two respects. First they must be
asked where the rationality is that they promised, where the
rejection of irrationality, where the expectation of knowledge:
"If it is wrong to believe anyone without proof, why are you
eager for me to believe someone without proof, in order for me
to be more easily led on by your reasoning? Will your rationality build something solid on a foundation of irrationality?" I am
speaking their language, as it is they who blame us for believing. I myself consider that, when you do not have the ability to
appreciate the arguments, it is very healthy to believe without
knowing the reasons and by that belief to cultivate the mind
and allow the seeds of truth to be sown. Moreover, for minds
that are ill this is absolutely essential, if they are to be restored
to health. Their view that this is ridiculous and quite irrational,
when in fact it is Christ in whom we believe, is insolent.

So I proclaim that I have already believed in Christ and instilled
into my mind that what he said is true, even if this is not shored
up by any proof. Are you, heretic, going to lead me on this basis?
Let me ponder a little. I have not actually seen Christ in the way he
chose to appear to the human race, although the teaching is that he
was visible even to the eyes of ordinary people. Whose testimony
about him is it that I have believed in order to come to you now
on the basis of that belief? I see that what I have believed is only

---

56. This verse of scripture was a favorite of the Manicheans; see *The Catholic Way of Life
and the Manichean Way of Life* II, 17, 31.

the accepted views and recognized traditions of communities and nations. Everywhere, however, these communities have been won over by the mysteries of the Catholic Church. Why, therefore, should I not look rather to them in my search for what Christ commanded, since it is already their testimony that has influenced me to believe that Christ commanded something of value? Are you going to give me a better account of what he said, even though I would not hold that he existed or exists if the advice to believe this had to come from you. As I said, I believed this because of the wide acceptance of the report, strong in its unanimity and antiquity.[57] No one doubts, however, that you, who are so few,[58] so new[59] and so confused, offer nothing worthy of credence. What insanity is this: "Believe them when they tell you that you should believe in Christ, but let us teach you what he said?" Why, I ask you? If they failed me and could not teach me anything, it would be easier to convince myself that I should not believe in Christ at all, rather than that I should learn anything about him other than from those through whom I had come to believe in him. What colossal confidence! Indeed, what colossal stupidity! "I shall teach you what Christ, in whom you believe, commanded," they say. "What? Would you be able to teach me about him, if I did not believe in him?" "But you should believe," they say. "Does that mean to believe in him because you commend him to us?" "No," they say, "because we guide by reason those who do believe in him." "Why, then, should I believe in him?" "Because it is reliably reported." "By you or by others?" "By others," they say. "Therefore I must believe them in order to be taught by you? Perhaps I should do that, except that they advise me particularly to have nothing to do with you, as they say your teachings are pernicious. You will answer that they are lying. But why then should I believe what they say about Christ, whom they have not seen, but not believe what they say about you, whom they do not want to see?" "Believe what is written," they say. "But any writing that is newly published and unknown, or is recommended by a few people with no supporting reasons, is

57. See *True Religion* 3, 5; *Faith in the Unseen* 3, 5.
58. See *The Catholic Way of Life and the Manichean Way of Life* II, 20, 75; *Answer to Secundinus* 36; *Answer to Faustus, a Manichean* XIII, 5; XX, 23.
59. All the same, about 115 years had passed since the death of Mani.

not accepted on its own merits but because of those who publish it. Therefore, if it is you who publish those writings, as few and unknown as you are, I am not inclined to accept them. At the same time you even break your own promise by demanding belief rather than giving reasons. You will refer me again to the masses and to reputation.

"In the end contain your obstinacy, and whatever uncontrolled lust for glory it is, and direct me instead to search out the leaders of these masses, and to search long and hard, in order to learn something about these writings from them instead. Without them I should not even know there was anything to learn. But you yourself go back to your lairs and do not lie in wait to snatch something in the name of the truth that you are trying to steal from those whose authority you yourself acknowledge."

32. If they say we should not even believe Christ without irrefutable proof, then they are not Christians. That is what some of the pagans say against us. It is certainly foolish of them, but at least they are not attacking or contradicting themselves. But who would allow these people to claim they belong to Christ when they argue that nothing should be believed until they have provided the unintelligent with a clear understanding of God? As we see from the teaching of that historical record, which even they accept, his own first and greatest wish was to be believed, because those with whom he was dealing were not yet ready to comprehend the divine mysteries. What else are those many great miracles doing, when he himself said the only reason for them was to bring people to believe in him? He led the foolish by faith; you lead them by reason. He called on us to believe in him; you call us back. He praised those who believe; you blame them. If we could follow those who do nothing of that nature but only teach, then either he did not turn water into wine[60] (not to mention other miracles), or no weight should be given to that utterance, *Believe in God and believe me* (Jn 14:1), or the one who did not want him to come to his home because he believed his son would be cured by his mere command[61] is guilty of irrationality.

---

60. See Jn 2:7-9.
61. See Mt 8:8.

So he who brought the remedy that would heal corrupted morals established authority with miracles, won belief with authority, held the masses with belief, endured through the masses, and made religion strong by enduring. The crude novelties of the heretics have failed to dislodge it in any way with their deceits, any more than did the violent opposition of the ancient errors of the pagans.

15, 33. For these reasons, even though I am not empowered to teach, I do not cease to advise. Since many want to appear wise, and it is not easy for the unwise to tell whether they really are, if your heart is set on a happy life, then with total commitment and every kind of offering, with sighs and even in tears if possible, pray to God to deliver you from the evil of error.

This will be more readily accomplished if you give willing obedience to his commandments, which he chose to support with the great authority of the Catholic Church. The wise person is so united in mind to God that nothing can come between to separate them, for God is truth and it is not possible for anyone to be wise whose mind is not in contact with the truth. Hence we cannot deny that human wisdom is interposed as a kind of intermediary between human foolishness and God's absolute truth. The wise person imitates God, to the extent that this is possible; the nearest thing the foolish can gainfully imitate is the wise person. Since, as we have said, it is not easy to discern this person by reason, certain miracles had to be presented for the eyes to see, which the foolish are better fitted to using than they are to using their mind. Then, by responding to authority, people would first have their lives and conduct purified and in that way grow capable of being given understanding.

Since, therefore, we had to model ourselves on a human being but not set our hopes on a human being, could God have done anything kinder or more generous than for the real, eternal, unchanging wisdom of God itself, to which we must cling, to condescend to take on human form? He would not only do the things that call us to God but would also suffer the things that turn us away from following God. No one can acquire the supreme and lasting good without loving it totally and unreservedly, and this is not possible as long as material evils and misfortunes inspire terror. By his miraculous birth and his deeds he won our love, but by his death and resurrection he drove out fear. In all the other things, which it would take a long time to go into, he showed himself for us to see how the divine mercy can reach out and human weakness be lifted up.

16, 34. Believe me, this authority is what saves us, this prior lifting of our mind from its earthly habitat, this turning from the love of this world to the true God. It is only authority that enables the foolish to move quickly to wisdom. As long as we are unable to understand reality, it is indeed a wretched thing to be misled by authority, but it is undoubtedly more wretched not to respond to it at all. If God's providence does not preside over human affairs, there is no need to be concerned at all about religion. If, however, the outward appearance of everything (which we surely must believe emanates from some source of true beauty)[62] and a certain inner consciousness combine, publicly and privately as it were, to urge all better minds to look for God and serve God, then we should not abandon hope that there is some authority established by that God himself to be like a fixed step on which we may stand to be lifted up to God.

Putting aside the reasoning that, as we have said repeatedly, is very hard for the foolish to understand in itself, this influences us in two ways: in part by the miracles, and in part because of its wide acceptance. No one denies that the wise person has no need for anything like this, but the present aim is to become capable of being wise, that is, able to be held by the truth. This is not possible for a mind that is defiled. What defiles the mind, if I may explain it briefly, is love of anything at all other than the mind itself and God. The more one is cleansed of this defilement, the more easily one discerns the truth. Since, therefore, your mind is purified in order for you to see the truth, it is obviously perverse and absurd to want to see the truth in order to purify your mind.

Hence authority is there for those who are incapable of gazing on the truth, so that they may become fit to do so by allowing themselves to be purified. No one doubts it has this power, partly because of the miracles and partly because of its wide acceptance, as I have just said. I call a miracle any event that is so difficult or

---

62. In Neoplatonic thought, being is hierarchically ordered. Each next lower level proceeds from the higher by "emanation" ("overflow") without any diminution occurring thereby to the higher.

extraordinary as to be beyond the expectation or power of those it astonishes. Under this heading nothing is more appropriate for people generally, and especially for foolish persons, than things that affect the senses. These in turn can be of two kinds. There are some that only inspire wonder, and some that also procure a great privilege and benefit. If we were to see someone flying,[63] that would bring no benefit to the spectator other than the actual spectacle, and we would merely be astonished. If, however, someone suffering from a serious and terminal illness recovers immediately when this is commanded, the charity of the person working the cure adds to the wonder at the cure.

This is what happened in those days when, as was required, God showed himself to the human race as a real human being. The sick were cured; lepers were cleansed; the lame were made to walk; sight was restored to the blind and hearing to the deaf.[64] The people of those times saw water changed into wine, five thousand people fed to fullness with five loaves, the seas crossed on foot, the dead restored to life.[65] Some of these things were more obviously for the good of the body, some were in more hidden fashion signs for the mind, but all were evidence to us of greatness. In this way the divine authority turned the straying souls of mortal men and women of those times towards itself.

Why, you say, do these things not happen now? Because they would not have any effect unless they caused wonder, and, if they were common occurrences, they would not cause wonder.[66] Think of the alternation of day and night and the undeviating pattern of the heavenly bodies, the four seasons of the year, the fall and return of the leaves of the trees, the infinite power of seeds, the beauty of light and colors and sounds and smells, and the variety of tastes. Imagine being able to talk to someone who saw and experienced these things for the first time. That person would be astonished and overwhelmed by the miracles. We, on the other hand, think

---

63. Augustine may have been thinking of Medea in flight, on whom he wrote declamations during his study of rhetoric (see *Confessions* III, 6, 11), or of Daedalus and Icarus (see *Soliloquies* II, 20; *Order* II, 37).

64. See Mt 11:5; 15:31.

65. See Jn 2:1-11; Mt 14:13-23; Mt 14:22-33; Mt 9:18-26; Lk 7:11-17; Jn 11:1-46.

66. See *Revisions* I, 14, 5: "By this I meant to say that nowadays there are no longer so many and such great miracles, but not that there are no miracles anymore."

little of all these things. It is certainly not because of any ease in understanding them, as nothing surely is more obscure than their explanation, but because it is a continual experience. These things were done, therefore, at the appropriate time, so that with the conversion and spread of so many believers authority would, because of them, become a beneficial influence on established morality.

17, 35. Any established morality holds such great power over people's minds that we are better able to condemn and detest any perversions in them, which happen because of the almost complete domination of sensuality, than to abandon them or change them. Do you think it matters little for humanity that so few scholars argue that nothing composed of earth or fire, in short nothing that the bodily senses can touch, should be worshiped as God, since God can only be apprehended by the intellect, yet the uneducated masses of men and women of many nations both believe this and preach it? Do you think it matters little that abstinence even from the tiniest morsel of bread and water, and not just fasting on single days but even fasting sustained over several successive days, is aspired to, and chastity even to the point of rejecting marriage and children, and endurance even to the point of ignoring crucifixion and fire, and generosity even to the point of distributing one's inheritance to the poor, in short, disdain for this world even to the point of desiring death? Few do these things, and even fewer do them well and wisely, but people everywhere approve of them, people everywhere praise them, people everywhere applaud them; in a word, people everywhere hold them in highest esteem. People blame their own frailty because they cannot do these things, but they do not do so without raising their minds towards God or without some spark of virtue.

This has been brought about by divine providence through the utterances of the prophets, through the humanity and teaching of Christ, through the journeys of the apostles, through the derision, crosses, blood and death of the martyrs, through the exemplary lives of the saints, and in all cases, as appropriate for the time, through miracles befitting such great deeds and virtues. When, therefore, we see such great help from God, so productive and so beneficial, shall we hesitate to hide in the bosom of his Church? From the apostolic throne,[67] through the chain of succession of the bishops, it occupies the pinnacle of authority, acknowledged by the whole human race. In vain do the heretics howl around her, condemned variously by the judgment of the ordinary people themselves, by the weight of authority of the councils, by the grandeur of miracles.

To refuse to acknowledge her primacy is assuredly either the height of sacrilege or the height of headstrong arrogance. If souls have no secure path to wisdom and salvation unless faith prepares the ground for understanding, is it anything but ingratitude for God's help and assistance if one chooses to resist such a strongly supported authority? If any subject, however lowly and easy to understand, requires a teacher or tutor, could there be anything more proud and reckless than to refuse to learn about the books of the divine mysteries from their interpreters and then to dare to condemn them without knowing anything about them?

18, 36. For these reasons, if either our reasoning or our pleading has any effect on you, and if, as I believe you do, you have any real concern for yourself, it is my wish that you will listen to me and commit yourself to the good teachings of Catholic Christianity, doing so with devout faith, lively hope and simple love, and that you will not cease to pray to God himself. It is only through his goodness that we were created, and only through his justice that we suffer punishment, and only through his mercy that we are set free. Then you will not lack either the guidance and commentary of great scholars who are also truly Christian, or the books, or the calm reflection itself, by means of which you will easily find what you are looking for.

Abandon completely those loquacious wretches—could I call them anything kinder? While they search too hard for the origin of evil,[68] they find nothing except evil. They often arouse their listeners to investigate this question, but, once aroused, what they teach them is such that it would even be better for them to

---

67. See *Answer to the Letter of Mani Known as "The Foundation"* 4.
68. *Malum*, used here, signifies both physical evil and moral wickedness.

sleep forever than to be awake like that. They change them from
drowsy to delirious,[69] and between the two maladies, although
both are usually fatal, there is the difference that the drowsy die
without causing trouble to others, whereas the delirious are a
danger to many healthy people, and especially to those trying
to help them. God is not the author of evil, and he never regrets
creating anything, and he does not become unsettled by any
storm of mental tumult, and his kingdom is not some portion of
the world, and he does not approve of any crime or atrocity, and
he never lies. These and similar assertions influenced us, when
they brandished them at us with great invective, claiming they
were the teachings of the Old Testament, though that is entirely
untrue.[70] I admit they were right to condemn those things. So
what did I learn? What do you think? Only that when those assertions are condemned the Catholic Church is not condemned.
So I retain the truth that I learned when I was with them, but I
repudiate the false opinions I held.

The Catholic Church, however, has taught me many other
things to which these people with their feeble bodies[71] and gross
minds cannot aspire: that God is not a material being and no part
of him can be perceived by the eyes of the body, that nothing of
his substance and nature is in any way corruptible or changeable
or composite or created. If you agree with me about this—and
God must not be thought of in any other way—all their machina-
tions are overturned. As for that other matter, however, how it is
that God did not generate or create evil, and also that there does
not exist and there never has existed any nature or substance
that God did not generate or create, and yet he delivers us from
evil: that is established by such compelling arguments that there
cannot be any doubt about it, especially for you and people like
you. Along with a good intellect, however, there must be a de-

---

69. This is possibly an allusion to the attacks on the name of Mani made in the Greek-
   speaking world. A play on words was often made between Manes, Mani's name in
   Greek, and *maneis*, i.e., "furious, raging, insane." See S. N. C. Lieu, "Some Themes in
   Later Roman Anti-manichean Polemics, 1," Bulletin of the John Rylands Library of
   Manchester 68 (1985-86) 440-441.
70. See *The Catholic Way of Life and the Manichean Way of Life* I, 10, 16.
71. "Feeble" because of the asceticism of the elect.

vout attitude and a certain calmness of mind, without which it is not possible to understand anything at all about such profound matters. We are not dealing here with some story about smoke and a Persian myth[72] of some kind, where it is enough to give ear with a quite childlike mind rather than one of any subtlety. Truth is far, far different from this and is not as the Manicheans so foolishly perceive it.

As, however, our present discussion has lasted much longer than I thought it would, let us conclude the book here. I should like you to note that in it I have not yet begun to refute the Manicheans and have not yet started on that trivia, nor have I expanded on anything of substance about the actual Catholic teaching. I only wanted to weed out from you, if I could, the false opinions about Christian truths that were instilled in us through malice or ignorance and to raise your mind to learn certain great truths about God. That is why this volume is as it is. Now that your mind has been made more receptive, I shall perhaps move along more rapidly regarding other matters. Amen.[73]

---

72. Mani was of Persian origin; see *Answer to Faustus, a Manichean* XXIV, 4; *Answer to Secundinus* 2.
73. On this concluding section see *Revisions* I, 14, 6.